3—

THE COLUMBUS PAPERS

REPRODUCTION OF CHRISTOPHER COLUMBUS'
EARLIEST KNOWN OFFICIAL SIGNATURE AS ADMIRAL
OF THE OCEAN SEA, FROM HIS MEMORIAL TO THE
CROWN ON THE SECOND VOYAGE, DATED
JANUARY 30, 1494 (PALACIO DE LIRIA, MADRID).

Columbus typically signed his name with the circular group of letters appearing to the upper left of "el almirant." *In the entail to his property he described this cryptogram as* "an X with an S over it and an M with a Roman A over it and over that an S, and then a Greek Y with an S over it, preserving the relationship of the lines and the points." *His meaning, however, remains a mystery. Morison interpreted the signature as a combination of Greek and Latin symbols meaning* Servant I am of The Most High Savior, Christ Son of Mary. *In other documents Columbus usually added the line* ":Xpo FERENS" *below the cryptogram, short for Christopher,* "the Christ Bearer."

S. S. S.
A.
Y M V

JCalderana

THE COLUMBUS PAPERS

The Barcelona Letter of 1493, the Landfall Controversy, and the Indian Guides

BY MAURICIO OBREGÓN

A FACSIMILE EDITION OF THE UNIQUE COPY IN THE NEW YORK PUBLIC LIBRARY,
WITH A NEW ENGLISH TRANSLATION BY LUCIA GRAVES

MACMILLAN PUBLISHING COMPANY   NEW YORK
MAXWELL MACMILLAN CANADA   TORONTO
MAXWELL MACMILLAN INTERNATIONAL
NEW YORK   OXFORD   SINGAPORE   SYDNEY

Macmillan Publishing Company   Maxwell Macmillan Canada, Inc.
866 Third Avenue   1200 Eglinton Avenue East
New York, NY 10022   Suite 200
                               Don Mills, Ontario M3C 3N1

Macmillan Publishing Company is part of the Maxwell Communication
Group of Companies.

Library of Congress Cataloging-in-Publication Data
Columbus, Christopher.
    [Carta (Feb. 18, 1493). English & Spanish]
    The Columbus papers: the Barcelona letter of 1493, the landfall
controversy, and the Indian Guides: a facsimile edition of the unique copy
in the New York Public Library / Mauricio Obregón / with a new English
translation by Lucia Graves.
        p.   cm.
    Includes bibliographical references.
    ISBN 0-02-591045-0
    1. Columbus, Christopher—Correspondence. 2. Columbus, Chris-
topher—Landfall.   3.   Explorers—America—Correspondence.   4.
Explorers—Spain—Correspondence.   5.   America—Discovery   and
exploration—Spanish. I. Graves, Lucia. II. Obregón, Mauricio. III. Title.
E115.2.E5C64   1991   91-19815   CIP
970.01′5—dc20

Line drawing maps courtesy of the author, drawn by Jim Haines.
Woodcuts courtesy of the New York Public Library, Rare Books and
Manuscripts Division and the Spencer Collection.

Macmillan books are available at special discounts for bulk purchases for
sales promotions, premiums, fund-raising, or educational use.
For details, contact:

Special Sales Director
Macmillan Publishing Company
866 Third Avenue
New York, NY 10022

10 9 8 7 6 5 4 3 2 1

PRINTED IN ITALY

CONTENTS

THE BARCELONA LETTER OF 1493,
THE LANDFALL CONTROVERSY,
AND THE INDIAN GUIDES

BY MAURICIO OBREGÓN

To my wife, Lita, who knows how to wait.

ACKNOWLEDGMENTS

My first acknowledgment goes to Samuel Eliot Morison, with whom I had the privilege of working, sailing, flying, and writing during many years.

My thanks also to Javier Obregón, whose cartography has proved indispensable; to my untiring secretary, Myriam de Correa; and to my shipmates Rafael Obregón, Hernán Echavarría, James F. Nields, Andrés Soriano, Maurice Baird-Smith, Roger Stone, and Captains Germán Castro and Pablo E. Cohen of the Colombian and Venezuelan Navies.

Many others helped me on my voyages, but they are too numerous to mention here; they know I never forget them.

I. Why Columbus?

O DISCOVER is to draw the veil. It is not to run into something and keep it to oneself. It is to push back the frontier of infinity and to pass the news on to posterity as part of its heritage. Just as today the discovery of life on another planet would change our universe, so the publication of Columbus's Barcelona Letter, announcing the Discovery, changed the face of the Renaissance globe. The "Indians" were, of course, already there, but they did not communicate their presence to the rest of the world; nevertheless we shall see that without them there would have been no Discovery. In historical times, Islam, the Vikings, and the Portuguese came close to discovering the New World, but all of them fell short.

After the death of the Prophet, to the cry of *Allahu Akbar* ("God is Great"), Islam hurled itself against its two great neighboring empires, Byzantium and Persia, and defeated them both. Three qualities made the Moslems invincible: the mobility of their warriors, who were almost as easy to support as their camels and mules; the keen blade of their holy war, to which the constant presence of God gave a sharpened sense of destiny; and their clemency toward the vanquished. Says the Koran: "Believe in God, and in what He has revealed to Abraham, Ishmael, Isaac, Jacob, Moses, Jesus and the Prophets: make no distinction between them, and submit only to Him." But one quality was missing: the magnificent lunacy needed to face the infinite Ocean. In 642, the second Caliph, Omar, turned west. He occupied Alexandria, and sent Ugba Ibn Nafi to overrun the south coast of the Mediterranean. "God is my witness that only the ocean's darkness has put a limit on what I have conquered in His name," cried he, as he rode his charger into the Atlantic surf off the beach at Agadir. The steady trade winds blew the foam to the west across the ocean, but Ibn Nafi did not notice.

The Moslems, together with the great Jewish cartographers, did complete most of the West's knowledge of Eurasia, from Spain to the Spice Islands, and of much of Africa, but they never dared to venture far into the "ocean's darkness." They calculated the circumference of the globe far better than Columbus, but they had no chronometer with which to measure longitude, so the single Continent which they bequeathed to the West seemed so broad that it left no room for America in the single Ocean which, they thought, washed both its extremes.

During the Middle Ages the Vikings spread terror in their slim warships, from Scandinavia to Sicily and from Ireland to the great rivers of Russia, while their peasant brothers, the Norsemen, followed their fortunes in beamy knarrs. They sailed west to Iceland and then to Greenland, and toward the end of the tenth century, Biarni Heriulfson set sail from Iceland for Greenland, drifted off his latitude, and came to a flat, rocky coast. He followed it to the northeast and returned to Greenland where he sold his knarr to Leif Ericsson, son of King Eric the Red. Leif decided to seek the timber which Greenland lacked in the land Biarni had sighted, and in the first summer of the eleventh century (the century of El Cid) he sailed west with thirty-five men. The Icelandic Sagas describe the coasts he explored. First Helluland, flat and rocky; then Markland, where spruce stood over long white beaches across which streams flowed into the sea; and finally Vinland, where Leif entered a shallow bay beyond a strait guarded by an island. In Vinland he built shelters where he stayed the rest of the summer and one winter; and in the spring he came home with a good cargo of wood. After Leif came Thorvald, then others. But dark barbarians in canoes, whom the Vikings called "Skrellings," soon attacked

Cover illustration of the ninth, and the first illustrated edition, of the Columbus letter.

Illustrations of the time were not intended as "picto-journalism," but as symbolic representations, and were often based on standard images. This woodcut represents the Santa María, *but is derived from an earlier cut in Breydenbach's* Peregrinationes in Terram Sanctam. . . , *Mainz, 1486. What the* Santa María *actually looked like is still a mystery.*

Christopher Columbus, Letter to Sanchez (Latin), Basel: Jacob Wolff, 1493 [It is a translator's error that the recipient is called Sanchez rather than Santángel.]

from the sea and sent them home. The Sagas say that in Vinland the sun shone longer than in Greenland, there was good pasture, and a salmon run flowed from a lake. Grapes or berries were so plentiful that Tyrker, Leif's German godfather, made wine and got drunk, thus giving Vinland its name. Today in Newfoundland, facing the Strait of Belle Isle, there is a grassy bay called Anse Aux Meadows, which is studded with blackberry bushes and watered by a stream which runs down from a lake. Here, the Norwegian archaeologist Helge Ingstad showed me the remains of shelters like those of Greenland, a few implements, and charcoal which has been dated to the eleventh century: This must be Vinland. Across the strait to the northeast there stretches a black and forbidding coast, where even in summer I have seen icebergs; but rounding Cape Porcupine near Hamilton Inlet, I suddenly found fifty kilometers of white beaches, where, from a beautiful stand of spruce, several streams flow into the sea; surely Markland. Finally, less than five degrees from the Arctic Circle, the rocky coast of Baffin Island seems perfect for Helluland.

The Vikings certainly hit upon Newfoundland, but the world at large did not hear of it, for the Sagas were not written down till the thirteenth century, and were only published in Latin in the eighteenth century. Vinland vanished, and the skeletons which have been found in Greenland are of small, undernourished people, apparently victims of the Little Ice Age which climatologists tell us froze their ports solid in the fifteenth century. America was not yet ready to spring its surprise.

With a population about to reach two million, while Britain's had just passed one million, fifteenth-century Portugal was Europe's prow, cutting into the ocean, and Portugal's Azores rode far ahead, one-third of the way to America. But the great Atlantic gyre decrees that the trade winds blow almost constantly on the Azores out of the west, so Portugal's advantage turned out to be her handicap in the race to the New World. From Sagres, near Cape St. Vincent in the Algarve (the Renaissance's Cape Canaveral), Prince Henry the Navigator sent Gonçalo Velho Cabral to discover the Azores in 1431, planting the Portuguese flag as far west as one needs to sail in order to return from Africa with the wind. Then several Portuguese captains dared double the eastern headlands of Africa: Cabo Bojador to the south of the Canaries, Cabo Verde where Dakar stands today, and Cabo Blanco midway between the two. Though it was still not known whether the equatorial sea boiled, King Alfonso V, Prince Henry's nephew, sent Fernan Gomes close to the equator, and Lope Gonçalves to cross it in 1475. Portugal also signed a treaty with Castile confirming the Papal Bull of 1454 which secured for Portugal a monopoly of the African coast. In 1488 Alfonso's son, João II, dispatched Bartolomeo Dias to round the Cape of Good Hope, and Vasco da Gama to Calicut (on the Malabar coast) via the Cape in 1497. From there the Portuguese, in the wake of Islam's dhows, advanced their caravels and their trading posts like pawns in a chess game, all the way to the Spice Islands.

Finally in 1500 Pedro Alvares Cabral, following da Gama's instructions to sail southwest in order to catch the wind to the Cape, hit upon Brazil's "bulge." But he baptized it "the island of Vera Cruz" and went his way.

So it fell to Spain and to Columbus to make the great leap. In 1492 Columbus was forty-one years of age and of good stature at a time when most men were short by our standards. His eyes were blue and his reddish hair prematurely graying. Always courteous, even with his crew, but as remote as he was religious, he cut an imposing figure. He signed himself "Christo Ferens," for he knew God had chosen him to carry the Cross to the Indies. He insisted vaguely on his high birth, though his grandfather Giovanni, his father Domenico, and his mother Susana Fontanarossa all came from a long line of weavers: This was the first of his three complexes, and what genius has no complexes? His second complex came from the way he looked out on the science of the Renaissance with the innocent eyes of the Middle Ages. Not satisfied with being the greatest intuitive sailor of all time, he strove to explain his navigation scientifically and failed; "Little do I like the reasons of this Admiral," said Peter Martyr, the Spanish Court's cosmographer. His third complex, persecution, would catch up with him later. Most important, he was a man with a single vocation. We have all met at least one of them: They are sometimes unbearable and sometimes irresistible. Such was Columbus, yet we shall see that he was human enough to fall in love, more than once.

He was born in southern Genoa in 1451, two years before the fall of Constantinople to the Turks, the same year as Queen Isabella, and one year before King Ferdinand. He himself and all his contemporaries attested that he was a Genoese, *Ligur Vir*. Nevertheless he was not exactly Italian, for Italy was not yet a nation-state, and Ligurians spoke a dialect unintelligible in the rest of the peninsula. Genoa was an amphitheater full of seagulls and sails, and while Christopher's hands worked at his family's looms, his soul filled with dreams of distant horizons. In his twenties, he sailed to the island of Chios where he learned that a single Genoese fort could dominate the trade of a whole region; and in 1476, he went out into the Atlantic with a Genoese convoy which was attacked and sunk by the infamous Guillaume de Casenove.

The future Discoverer reached the beach at Lagos in Portugal clinging to an oar, then joined his brother Bartholomew, two years his junior but already working as a mapmaker in Lisbon. In Portugal he learned to write in Spanish, the language of the court, and married Felipa

Moñíz de Perestrello, daughter of the Governor of Porto Santo, Madeira. We know little of Felipa, but we imagine her fine and frail, for she was an aristocrat who in 1480 gave birth to Diego, Columbus' only legitimate heir, then died. With the Portuguese, Columbus sailed well north of the Azores, where the wind almost always blows out of the west, then to Madeira, where the wind blows steadily out of the north, and then to West Africa, where he surely observed what Ibn Nafi had not noticed, that there the wind blows constantly toward the west. So he discovered the Atlantic gyre, which decrees that trade winds (and currents) circle clockwise around the north Atlantic. If he had a secret this was it: He knew how to sail west to the Indies and, more important, how to return. But Portuguese cosmographers knew that East Asia could not be as close as Columbus thought, and Columbus failed to sell them his project.

Much of Columbus' geography came from Marco Polo, whose memoirs were in Columbus' library, and whose enthusiastic prose described Cathay and the Malay straits which Columbus later sought in Central America. Columbus thought that the circumference of the globe was smaller than Eratosthenes had successfully calculated three centuries before Christ. While sailing south from Lisbon to Guinea, he reckoned the length of a degree at fifty-six and two-thirds of his miles. This gave him a circumference of twenty thousand four hundred of his miles, equivalent to fifteen thousand three hundred of our nautical miles, about three-quarters of the true circumference. In addition, Columbus loved to quote the Prophet Esdras who said that only one-seventh part of the globe was covered by water, so he calculated that Asia reached much farther around the globe than it does. All this left only some three thousand nautical miles of ocean between Europe and Asia. Paolo Toscanelli, the Florentine physician and cosmographer, sent Columbus a copy of a letter he had earlier sent to Canon Martins, in which he confirmed Columbus' views: "From the island of Antillia, which you know, to the noble island of Cipangu, there are two thousand five hundred miles, so it is not necessary to traverse a great stretch of sea by unknown routes." Toscanelli's map disappeared, but it was probably similar to Behaim's globe of 1492, which gives us a good idea of how the world looked to Columbus' educated contemporaries, although Columbus probably did not see it before he sailed. In our illustration we compare it with Juan de la Cosa's map of 1500; the world just before the discovery, and just after it.

In 1485 Columbus moved to Spain, where Seville with its great port on the river Guadalquivir was rapidly becoming the capital of the Castilian ocean. While waiting for the Queen's itinerant Court in Córdoba, Columbus, now a widower, fell in love with Beatriz Henriquez de Arana, about whom we know as little as we do about Felipa, Columbus' wife. But we imagine her as handsome and ample, a woman of the people whom the ambitious Columbus dared not marry, but who during Columbus' voyages looked after both Felipa's Diego and her own Fernando, to whom she gave birth in 1488. Although illegitimate, Fernando was to be Columbus' most important son, his first biographer, and a bibliophile who left us many of Columbus' annotated books.

Spanish cosmographers knew as well as their Portuguese colleagues that Asia lay three times as far to the west as Columbus claimed. Little did they know that America, that continental surprise, lay just about where Columbus figured Asia would begin. Characteristically, Columbus was wrong but right. Just in time, Luis de Santángel, King Ferdinand of Aragon's Secretary of the Treasury, reminded Queen Isabella that she had nothing to lose; he would finance the voyage out of the coffers of Aragon, and the town of Palos would supply the ships. The Queen knew how important it was that

Spain, accustomed to centuries of conflict, should continue pushing forward its frontiers, now no longer against the Moors at home but across the ocean. I am sorry to say that she did not in fact have to pawn her jewels; but it was certainly her vision, King Ferdinand's money, and Christopher Columbus' stubbornness which launched the enterprise.

In the spring of 1492, immediately after the surrender of Granada, the King and Queen signed Columbus' hard-won *Capitulaciones*, his sailing contract. It granted him the title of Admiral, which his descendants still bear, and made him Viceroy of all the lands he might discover, a post which he would soon lose. It also granted him a tenth of all treasure found, a privilege he retained until his death; but which, as we shall see, he and the King interpreted very differently.

The great voyage was on its way, and the first news of its success was to be Columbus' Barcelona Letter, which probably arrived at Court even before Columbus did; certainly before his Journal, which he may well have delivered to the Catholic Sovereigns, but which we know only from the transcription that the Franciscan bishop Bartolomé de Las Casas wrote into his *Historia* more than half a century after the Discovery, and which was not published until 1875. So it was the letter, published almost immediately, which launched the Age of Discovery. For Europe, it was the birth certificate of America.

The sole extant copy of the Barcelona Letter, the rarest and most important single document in the annals of Americana, as Samuel Eliot Morison called it, is in the New York Public Library. Columbus addressed it to Luis de Santángel from Lisbon on the day of his return from his first voyage, and within a few weeks it had been printed by Pedro Posa in Barcelona, where the Court was in session. In those days presses normally creaked, but Columbus' letter made them buzz; a dozen editions

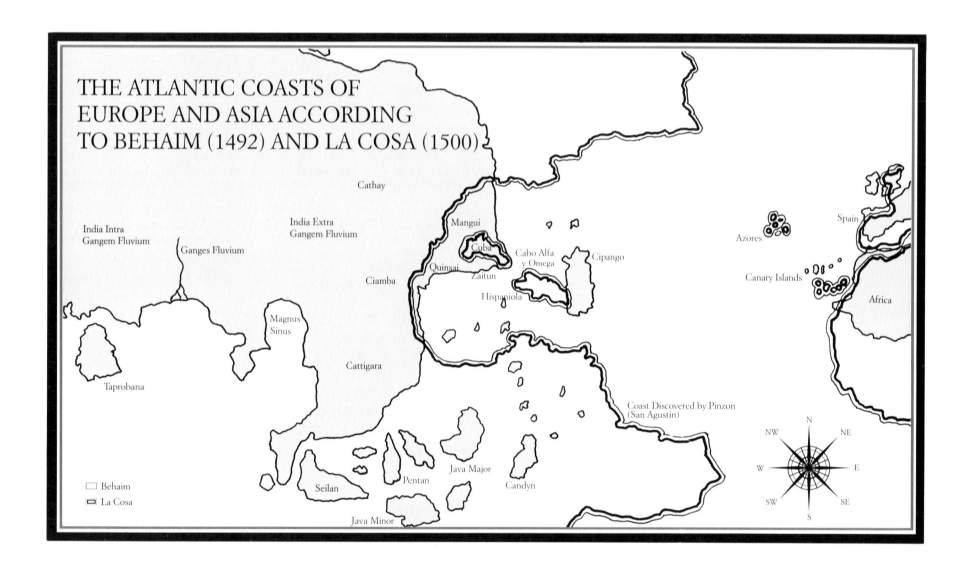

THE ATLANTIC COASTS OF
EUROPE AND ASIA ACCORDING
TO BEHAIM (1492) AND LA COSA (1500)

Cathay

India Intra
Gangem Fluvium

India Extra
Gangem Fluvium

Mangui

Spain

Ganges Fluvium

Cuba

Azores

Cabo Alfa
y Omega

Cipango

Quinsai

Zaitun

Ciamba

Hispaniola

Canary Islands

Magnus
Sinus

Africa

Cattigara

Taprobana

Coast Discovered by Pinzon
(San Agustin)

N

NW   NE

W   E

Java Major

Pentan

Seilan

Candyn

SW   SE

Java Minor

S

☐ Behaim
⊟ La Cosa

appeared within a year of his return, in three languages. The manuscript disappeared along with many of Columbus' other writings, and the copy of the Posa edition was only rediscovered in 1889, by the Paris dealer J. Maisonneuve, who sold it to the London dealer Bernard Quaritch. In 1891 Quaritch circulated a black-and-white facsimile as a selling piece, then sold the copy to the estate of the American collector James Lenox, who had willed his collection to the founding of the New York Public Library.

Lucia Graves' translation of the letter is, as far as I know, the first published since Samuel Eliot Morison's of 1956. It is based solely on the Posa printing, not on the standard transcription into modern Spanish. At first reading the letter may seem naive, but it is clear, lyric, matter-of-fact and brief, virtues uncommon then, and rarer still today. The Admiral begins by saying: "I discovered a great many islands inhabited by people without number: and of them all I have taken possession on behalf of Their Highnesses by proclamation and with the royal flag extended, and I was not opposed." No doubts here about his rights; he is putting his best foot forward, and he promises his sovereigns all kinds of riches: spices, gold, mastic, aloe, rhubarb, and cinnamon. He does not mention his differences with Martín Alonso Pinzón, Captain of the *Pinta*, nor does he say anything of the loss of his flagship, the nao *Santa María*, near today's Cap Haitien, except that the ships had not "served me as it would have been reasonable to expect." He merely states that he built a fort there, at Navidad, where he left some forty men. Typically rationalizing, he even extols the virtues of the place, as if he has chosen it: "It is situated in the most convenient spot on the island and in the best district for gold mines and for all kinds of trade with the nearest mainland as well as with the farther one of the Great Khan." He thinks the forty men will be quite safe if they govern wisely,

which apparently they did not, for all died at the hands of the "timid" Indians, who soon found out that the Spaniards did not come from heaven.

Columbus tells how he landed in the Bahamas and how he named them, then goes straight on to Cuba (Isla Juana) which first seemed to him to be Terra Firma, perhaps the Asian province of Cathay, but which turned out to be a very large island, just as his Indian guides had indicated. Cuba, says Columbus, is the most beautiful island; but his real love is the next island, Hispaniola, which he describes in the most glowing terms: harbors, rivers, mountains, trees, birds, and beautiful Indians. He says that the people of all these islands go naked, men and women alike; they are of handsome build and unbelievably generous with what they have; and they do not know any sect or idolatry. No monsters here, he says, laying Sir John Mandeville to rest. But he has heard that on Matinino (Martinique), "the first island from Spain," there are Amazons, and that on Carib (probably Dominica), "the second island," there are cannibals, who "have many canoes with which they have the run of all the islands . . . and use bows and arrows." On his second voyage he will make his landfall on this island, an amazing feat of navigation.

We shall see that the letter is also important because it clears up several points of navigation which are unclear in Columbus' Journal, for example the latitude of the northern coasts of Cuba and Hispaniola, and the distance between the two islands (eighteen leagues). The apparent exaggeration of the figures that Columbus gives in the letter for the length of the coasts of the two great islands has led to the proposal that Columbus might have used two kinds of leagues; an intriguing hypothesis but a difficult one for a navigator to accept. Along the Cuban coast Columbus first sailed west for a day, then back east to Rio de Mares, and then he tried for two long weeks to reach Baneque (Great Inagua) without success, returning every time to a different part of the coast of Cuba. Consequently, his total exploration could indeed have been quite long. As to the coast of Hispaniola, it took Columbus a month to run the length of it against the current, almost always beating against the prevailing trade wind, so he can perhaps be forgiven for his overestimation of the distance covered. Anyone who has spent most of the months of December and January bucking the trades along this coast, as I have, will understand. The Admiral ends his letter by saying that God has given him this apparently impossible victory because he has walked in His ways, unlike others, who have tried to describe these lands in words, not in deeds. And he adds that in the Indies "not only Spain but all Christendom will find solace and profit"; truer even than he could dream, as millions upon millions of immigrants of all religions will confirm today.

Columbus' faith had proved unshakable, and faith can, and often does, overrule science. Columbus had done what the Moslems dared not do, what the Norsemen never realized, and what Portugal just missed: He had breached the ocean. Unlike the Vikings, Columbus was not satisfied with bumping into new lands without identifying them; he had torn aside the veil and described what he had found, and in the letter he hurried to propose a second voyage, for which he soon assembled seventeen ships. He would complete his discovery, and bequeath it to the Renaissance, which needed to paint, to sculpt, to sing, to possess the whole wide world, but could not have done it without Columbus' letter.

II. How Columbus Sailed

We still have no complete description of a fifteenth-century caravel or "nao," which simply means big ship, but we do have Columbus' description of *Santa María's* rigging, and we know that *Niña* was rerigged by Co-

lumbus with a square mainsail, the better to run with the wind. With Frédéric Dumas, Jacques Cousteau's underwater archaeologist, I searched unsuccessfully for Columbus' last caravels in St Ann's Bay, Jamaica, where he beached and abandoned them, and the Institute for Nautical Archaeology is continuing our work. On Molasses Reef, off Turks and Caicos, what may be the remains of a caravel have been found; the Italians are investigating a wreck off Sardinia which appears to be of the time of Columbus, and the Spaniards another in Culip, on the Costa Brava; remains of caravels should eventually turn up at Ysabela in the Dominican Republic, and at Rio de Belén and Portobello, in Panama; and many of us have tried to locate the wreck of *Santa María* near Cap Haitien, so far without success. In the meantime, we have to rely on experts like José María Martínez Hidalgo who have pieced together information from nautical manuals, from illustrations on old charts, and also from the "Mataró ship," the only contemporary model in existence, which unfortunately represents neither a nao nor a caravel.

The nao *Santa María*, also called "La Gallega" because she was built in Galicia, displaced about a hundred *toneles*, some one hundred and twenty tons, for the number of *toneles* was not the ship's total displacement but the number of 290-gallon barrels (or "tuns") of wine which could be carried, a tradition started by the Greeks with their ship-borne amphoras of wine and oil. She measured somewhat more than twenty-five meters on the waterline and nearly eight meters on the beam, and drew some two meters. She carried a large squaresail on her mainmast, which was twenty-seven meters high, a small topsail above the maintop tower, a lateen sail on the mizzenmast on her poop, a small squaresail on the foremast, and a spritsail under the bowsprit.

Pinta, built in Andalucía, was a caravel of about sev-

"The People of the Islands Recently Discovered . . ."

Native Americans had been brought back to Europe from as early as 1493 but the figures represented are those of naked Europeans. The frame house and the figures, particularly the standing figure with the bow, clearly have their origin in Albrecht Dürer's woodcut of circa 1476, "The Bath-House" (B. 348). The written description derives, probably at second or third hand, from Sir John Mandeville's mid fourteenth century account of the Far East.

Woodcut with coloring, Augsburg or Nuremberg, circa 1505.

enty *toneles*, some twenty meters on the waterline, some six meters on the beam, and with a draught of less than two meters. She carried a square mainsail and a lateen on her poop.

Niña, or *Santa Clara*, also Andalusian, was a slightly smaller caravel and a good sailor. Columbus' favorite, she was the only one of the original ships to make two more voyages to America after the Discovery. She started with a classic Portuguese lateen rig, but in the Canary Islands she was rerigged like *Pinta* for faster downwind sailing, which confirms that Columbus was already planning to follow the trades around the Atlantic, to the Indies and back.

On October 20, 1492, and again on November 22, when Martín Alonso Pinzón deserted the Admiral, Columbus' Journal confirms that the caravels were faster than the nao, and I submit that this was so, not only because they were slimmer, but because they were double-ended under the waterline, whereas the nao was beamy and had a blunt stern. According to the Journal, the fleet's speed often reached twelve Roman miles per hour in the open sea and with a good following wind; that is nine knots, good speed even for a modern yacht. The Journal of October 8 gives us a maximum figure of fifteen Roman miles, twelve knots; but it appears that even Las Casas thought that was too much, for he adds "if the text does not lie." All three ships carried fixed ballast of mortar and loose stones; all were completely decked and had forecastles and sterncastles except for *Niña*, which had no forecastle, so that her original lateen yardarm could come across the bow. Below the castles two thick beams pierced the hulls; they were called *Catenas*, and were probably used for towing. I think these beams descend directly from Argo's *threnos*, which was used to secure lines, and as a step. The traditions of the sea change slowly. The crew lists are interesting, especially because they include three names which would for a long time figure high in the annals of discovery: Vicente Yañez Pinzón would discover the Amazon; Juan de la Cosa would draw the first map of America and cross the ocean six times; and Pero Alonso Niño, at the same time as Ojeda, would explore the Spanish Main.

Nao Santa María
Captain: Christopher Columbus
Pilot: Pero Alonso Niño
Master and Owner: Juan de la Cosa
Marshal: Diego de Arana
Scribe: Rodrigo de Escobedo
Interpreter: Luis de Torres
Surgeon: Juan Sánchez
Veedor (literally "Overseer"): Rodrigo Sánchez de Segovia
Seven petty officers, captain's steward and page, eleven able seamen and ten *grumetes* (ship's boys).

Caravel Pinta
Captain: Martín Alonso Pinzón
Pilot: Cristóbal García de Sarmiento
Owner: Cristóbal Quintero
Marshal: Juan Reynal
Surgeon: Maestre Diego
Two petty officers, ten able seamen and eight *grumetes*.

Caravel Niña
Captain: Vicente Yáñez Pinón
Pilot: Sancho Ruiz de Gama
Master and Owner: Juan Niño
Marshal: Diego Lorenzo
Surgeon: Maestre Alonso
Two petty officers, eight able seamen and six *grumetes*.

Life on board the ships was at best spartan; I know, because I have sailed on the first high-seas voyage of the reproductions built by Spain for the Five-hundredth Anniversary. On *Santa María* the Admiral had a cabin to himself in the stern castle while most of the others slept wherever they could, but even the cabin was hardly a comfortable place to sleep; it was so high that it rocked terribly, and below it creaked the great tiller, held in place with block and tackle. As far as I know, Sebastian Cabot, scoundrel son of John, was the first to bring along a cook; before that, salted meat, fish, flour, and chickpeas were prepared by the crew over coals in an iron box under the fo'csle, eaten in any relatively cozy corner, and washed down with watered wine while it lasted, then with rotting water until rain could be caught in a sail. Mealtime conversation surely concentrated on things most missed: women, citrus fruit, and green vegetables. As to the body's necessities, they were done while swinging over the gun'l, and certainly not to the windward. Spanish sailors called the swing *el jardín* (the garden), a splendid euphemism which still means "the head." Not a comfortable life, but not much worse than that of any peasant of the time, and relieved by the beautiful traditions of the sea, especially by songs such as the one sung out each half hour when the hourglass was turned (hence our ship's bells): *Bendito sea el día en que Dios nació, San Juan que lo bautizó, y Santa María que lo parió*; and the Salve Regina, sung at sundown under the leadership of Columbus to much the same tune as we use today; everyone on the modern caravels claimed to have forgotten it, but when I started singing, one after the other joined in.

Columbus' basic system of navigation was dead reckoning: direction, speed, and elapsed time. Direction was measured with a compass which was divided into thirty-two points instead of our three-hundred-and-sixty degrees. So, theoretically, when translating compass points into degrees, there could be differences of up to 11¼ degrees, though in fact it is never necessary to apply such large corrections to Columbus' figures. Speed was estimated by the time it took a bow-wave or a floating object to travel the length of the ship. Three-fifths of the waterline in feet divided by the number of seconds gives the speed in knots; I have tried it with a champagne cork, and reached a reasonable approximation. Time was measured with a half-hour sand-glass; Columbus' Journal says so on December 13, 1492, and again on January 17, 1493. As Columbus points out on December 13, a seasick cabin boy might easily delay turning it, so the hour given by the sum of the half hours was at best approximate. It could be corrected at high noon, but only to local time. At night, Columbus obtained another rough estimate of time by watching the rotation of the "Guards" in the Big Dipper.

All this is not to say that the data contained in Columbus' Journal should be regarded as grossly inexact; but it does show that to try to crank exact information out of Columbus' Journal into a computer and draw exact conclusions, as some have done, is out of the question.

On October 13, 1492, Columbus says that San Salvador lies "east-west" of Fierro, the last of the Canaries, "under one line," and in his account of his third voyage, he confirms that in his first voyage he followed "the parallel of the Canaries." Moreover, in his third voyage Columbus says that when the North Star stood at five degrees, he planned to sail west instead of going farther south. All this suggests that Columbus supplemented his dead reckoning with latitude sailing, a method which had been used since the days of the ancient Greeks and Polynesians, for even with the naked eye it is not difficult to stay within a few degrees of a given latitude by the stars (again, I have tried it with reasonable success). When Columbus sailed in 1492, the Pleiades, or Seven

"The Spanish Island." Frontispiece of the first illustrated edition of the Columbus letter. The woodcut shows Europeans going ashore from a galley, a type of vessel which was completely unsuitable for any transatlantic voyage.

Christopher Columbus, Letter to Sanchez (Latin), Basel 1493

"The Spanish Island." Conventional representation of a Rhineland port town used to illustrate Columbus' description of the fort of Navidad.

Christopher Columbus, Letter to Sanchez (Latin), Basel 1493

Sisters, sailed with him, roughly along his latitude.

At least four times, Columbus tried to measure latitude by sighting the North Star with his quadrant. On October 30, and November 2 and 21, 1492, his Journal placed the north coast of Cuba at forty-two degrees North, when in fact it lies at just over twenty-one degrees; and on December 13 it places the latitude of the north coast of Hispaniola at thirty-four degrees, when in fact it lies at just over nineteen and a half degrees. On November 21, 1492, he even expressed doubts about the instrument itself, though it is the simplest of all nautical instruments; it consists of a quarter circle of wood or brass whose side one aims at the star, in order to measure the angle with the plumb line which hangs from its center. I have measured latitude to within a couple of degrees with a reproduction of a fifteenth-century quadrant. The Barcelona Letter solves the problem: In it Columbus corrects the Journal's major errors in latitude by saying that the latitude of the north coast of Hispaniola was twenty-six degrees North, which leaves an error of only five degrees.

Longitude is much more difficult to pin down. As the Earth rotates and latitudes circle faithfully under their own stars, longitudes tick around under the heavens like a monstrous clock, at the equator at about the speed of sound. Consequently, in order to calculate one's longitude by the stars, one needs to know the exact time at zero longitude (today, Greenwich), and to use an accurate chronometer, a sextant, and good tables. Columbus' sandglass (or the "Guards") and his quadrant were hardly adequate. Nevertheless, the Journal of January 13, 1493, tells us that the Admiral planned to observe the conjuction of the Moon, the Sun, and Mercury on the 17th , that is, to note when all three stood in the same longitude. He apparently knew that the difference between the local time of the conjunction and its European time as shown in Regiomontanus' *Ephemerides As-*

tronomicae would give him his relative longitude (hours multiplied by fifteen equals degrees of longitude), and it makes good sense that he should try to check his longitude before weighing anchor for Spain.

Las Casas, betraying his ignorance of navigation (not a required course for a bishop), thought Columbus was checking for "great winds," and he did not transcribe the result of the experiment, which could not have been good. According to Columbus' letter in his *Book of Prophecies*, on the 14th of September, 1494, he had another opportunity to use the same method on the island of Saona, by timing an eclipse of the moon, and another in Jamaica on February 29, 1504, but he never did achieve even an approximate estimate of longitude. So it seems clear that, though Columbus may have followed approximate latitudes, he could only estimate his east-west position by dead reckoning, and we shall see that he did pretty well.

The compass needle does not always point to true north and this magnetic variation (or declination) changes with position and with time. Scientific estimates, such as those by Jeremy Bloxham[1] of the Hoffman Laboratory at Harvard, indicate that in 1492 the magnetic variation along most of Columbus' transatlantic course ranged between zero degrees and ten degrees West, which fits the fact that the course from Fierro in the Canaries to San Salvador in the Bahamas runs some five degrees south of true west. On September 17, and again on September 30, 1492, Columbus noted in the Journal that, relative to the North Star, his compass needle seemed to deviate "one quarter" (some $11\frac{1}{4}$ degrees). In both cases he concluded that it was the North Star which moved, not the compass needle; very reassuring for his crews, for whom the compass was a lifeline. Today, the position of the North Star relative to

[1] "The Evolution of the Earth's Magnetic Field" (with David Gubbins), *Scientific American*, December 1989.

our Pole varies less than one degree, but because the earth, as it spins, wobbles slowly like a top, five hundred years ago the North Star's position varied close to seven degrees (almost three and a half each way), to which, in mid-Atlantic, magnetic variation would have to be added when the two variations coincided. So Columbus' observation and his conclusion were, once again, half right and half wrong, and it is clear that in his first voyage he did not correct for variation; nor in his third, when he noted even greater discrepancies between North Star and needles, but drew no conclusions at all. All in all, we can safely assume that he followed his compass.

Knowing one's ship, one can reasonably guess leeway, the ship's departure from course being steered, but Columbus ran free with the trade winds as he sailed west across the Atlantic, so his leeway was negligible. The trades are produced by the global heat-engine and the rotation of the earth, which have not changed significantly in five hundred years. In the tropics, warm air rises like a hot-air balloon, and in the polar regions it cools and drops back toward the earth. This creates a circulation in which air flows towards the equator on the surface, while, at altitude, it flows away from it, but the rotation of the earth deflects these great winds, and where there are large expanses of ocean, the trades take up a circular motion. This is the "Atlantic gyre," which flows clockwise in the north Atlantic, and anticlockwise in the south.

Currents follow similar patterns, and one can detect changes by watching the angle of the ship's wake. In a calm, one can dip the lead below surface currents and note the angle of the line. These methods are, of course, extremely approximate, and there is no evidence that Columbus used them, but it is an interesting coincidence that when he estimated current in mid-Atlantic, he was becalmed. During his first Atlantic crossing Co-

lumbus recorded two different sets of daily distances covered, and Las Casas says he did so in order to keep his crew from worrying that they had gone too far to get back. But it seems to me that, beginning with the brothers Pinzón, there were too many good navigators on board for such a deception to have gone unchallenged, and in any case the difference, which varied from day to day, averaged only about 13 percent, hardly enough to tranquilize a restless crew. Columbus' higher total figure, which he confirms on November 2, 1492, is approximately the distance from the Canaries to the Bahamas, and his lower total is some three hundred nautical miles less. The westward currents which dominate that part of the ocean average nearly half a knot, and in thirty-three days' sailing their effect would come pretty close to this difference. So it seems to me that Columbus may well have been estimating the help he was getting from the current. Be that as it may, the fact is that, according to the Journal, he often did take the current into account, not only when sailing along a coast, where it is relatively easy, but also when away from land. For instance, on September 17 and on December 5, 1492, his Journal says that the current helped the ships along; on September 13 and October 15, 1492, it says the current was against them; and on September 25, and again on November 20, it says that the current had set the ships to the northeast and to the northwest respectively.

In those days, each region had its favorite units of measurement, as did seafarers. This has led to a great deal of theoretical discussion as to the units Columbus used, but I prefer to base equivalences, not on theory, but on actual cases given in the Journal. As the fleet sailed on August 3, 1492, the Journal says: "'Til sunset we sailed south for sixty miles, which is fifteen leagues," and this four-mile league turns up more than a dozen times in the Journal. But the question remains: What was the length of Columbus' mile? On December 9,

1492, the Journal says that one thousand paces is a quarter of a league, so it is clear to me that Columbus used a league which contained four Roman miles of one thousand paces each. And each Roman pace, apparently measured at a run by some unfortunate Roman slave, is generally accepted to have been equivalent to one and a half meters, so each of Columbus' leagues was approximately equivalent to six kilometers, which is a little over three nautical miles. The three-nautical-mile league is confirmed by the Journal in the only two passages which describe long courses without interruption. From Palos to just before sighting the Canaries, with only two obvious extrapolations, the daily distances given in the Journal for August 3 to 8, 1492 add up to one hundred and fifty-four leagues, while the actual distance is some five hundred nautical miles. And the daily distances given for August 15 to 19, 1498, for the voyage diagonally across the Caribbean from Margarita to Isla Beata, Hispaniola, add up to one hundred and ninety-eight leagues, while the actual distance is some six hundred nautical miles. In both cases Columbus' league is equivalent to three nautical miles or a little more.

The great adventure which would lift the veil that still separated one half of the globe from the other started on May 23, 1492, at Palos. In front of the church of Saint Francis, Friar Juan Perez, who, with Friar Antonio Marchena, both of La Rábida, had been essential to the success of Columbus' idea, read the royal decree ordering the city of Palos to honor its obligations to the Crown by providing Columbus with two caravels. While the Pinzón brothers began recruiting the first ninety adventurers (only two jailbirds signed up, and the others must have been difficult to convince!), a nao from Galicia sailed into port and Columbus chartered it from Juan de la Cosa and signed him on as Master; he was to make half a dozen trips to America, draw the first map of the new world, and leave his bones in Cartagena,

Colombia. So, at dawn on Friday, August 3, 1492, where the rivers Odiel and Tinto meet to form the Saltés, three ships whose names will never be forgotten put out to sea, bound for the Canaries.

Columbus had made but one vow, to cross the Ocean, and on the Canary Island of Gomera, while *Pinta* had her rudder repaired on Gran Canaria (Columbus suspected that Quintero had damaged it in order to stay on the safe side of the Ocean), he fell in love with Beatriz de Bobadilla, daughter of Inés de Peraza, widow of the first Captain General of the island. The Admiral was *"Tincto d'amore"* on his first voyage, says Michele de Cuneo, the cheerful Genoese who also tells us that Columbus was again welcomed by Beatriz on his second voyage. But Columbus had more important things to do than remarry, and all he noted in his Journal was that Beatriz saw "land to the west of the Canaries every year." Nevertheless, the Bobadilla clan was not easy to ignore: Another Bobadilla later put Columbus in chains, and yet another married Pedrarias, who beheaded Balboa.

The story of Beatriz is worth telling, and it needs no embellishment. At court she was a ravishing beauty, and the Queen soon noticed that King Ferdinand's practiced eye had fallen on her. To hand came an amorous courtier named Hernán Peraza de Ayala y Rojas, and before he knew what hit him, the Queen had given him Inés in marriage, and named him Governor of Gomera, the outermost of the inhabited Canaries, in other words the end of the world. Once there, Peraza, not satisfied with one beauty (who is?), began to pursue the daughter of the local Guanche chief (Guanches were the Canaries' "Indians"). She led him into a trap, he was killed, and Beatriz was left to govern the island.

On Thursday, September 6, the fleet weighed anchors from Gomera, but on the northern limit of the trades the wind is variable, and it took three days to lose sight of Fierro, the westernmost of the Canaries, and of the Teide, the four-thousand-meter-high volcano that crowns Tenerife. On Saturday the 8th the wind finally made up its mind, and the fleet set sail.

Once in the trades, the first Atlantic crossing was a pure delight. With a following wind and the salt flavor of the unknown on his lips, Columbus had only to sail west along the latitude he had chosen, 28° N, the latitude of the Canaries, of the legendary Antillia, and of Cipangu (Japan). In the calm sea the fish played in safety, for the Spaniards did not fish much, just as for a long time they would not plant much in America; to discover is one thing, to work, another. The faithful wind sang in the rigging, and the sky, blue as God originally painted it, was dotted with small white cumulus clouds. Columbus wrote that the weather was like April in Andalusia. Nothing in this life is so sweet, not even final success, as the realization that one is embarked on one's chosen course.

On the sixteenth of September the expedition entered the Sargasso Sea, the hub of the Atlantic gyre, where so much flotsam accumulates (today it is largely plastic bottles) that the crews thought it might be an island. They saw "pigeons," dolphins, a whale, and a "fork-tailed bird which makes pelicans disgorge their food in the air in order to eat it itself," an exact description of the frigate bird (*Fregata aquila*), so common in the Caribbean, which I have sometimes caught at its tricks. Was this Antillia? Again on September 25, "in a sea like a river, in which many sailors went swimming," Martín Alonso Pinzón thought he saw land. How easy it is to see land on the high seas!

October came in with rain but no land, and within a week a worried Martín Alonso Pinzón began to consult with Columbus. The crews were getting restless; on several occasions they had made eight or nine knots or more downwind, and the estimate of the total distance

run made them wonder about getting back. But the wind did not encourage them to go about, and Columbus was the only one who knew in which part of the ocean the homeward winds blew. Besides, Pinzón had seen birds flying to the south-southwest, so Columbus gained a breathing space by promising to turn back if no land was sighted in three days.

Even as he approached it, Columbus fell in love with the Caribbean. In the Journal of October 8 he says, "The sea is as quiet as if it were a river, and the air is as sweet as it is in April in Seville, so fragrant that it is a joy to breathe." And later: "Only the song of the nightingale is missing.... The fish are so different from ours that it is a wonder. There are some like roosters, of the most delicate colors in the world, blue, yellow, red ... and others mottled in a thousand different ways.... There are oaks and evergreens ... and the song of the birds is so sweet that a man could never wish to leave this place, with its flocks of parrots which ... darken the sun."

On Thursday, October 11, signs of land appeared on the water. The moon rose late, and at ten o'clock Columbus saw a light that oscillated on the horizon. Pedro Gutierrez saw it too, but Rodrigo Sanchez de Segovia, the King's "overseer," did not; a good bureaucrat. At two in the morning Rodrigo de Triana's cry of *"Tierra!"* was heard from *Pinta*, and Martín Alonso Pinzón confirmed that land was visible in the moonlight. It seems that Columbus split with Pinzón the ten thousand maravedís promised by the King to the first man to sight land in the Indies (a sailor made twelve thousand maravedís a year). Rodrigo de Triana earned only a silk waistcoat, and, though Oviedo says he went to Africa and became a Moslem, he eventually sailed into the Pacific with Loayza and Elcano, where all three died of scurvy.

The Admiral, and he was Admiral now by right, was

Woodcut showing a caravel sailing from a fortified town before a conventional schematic representation of the islands that Columbus names in the letter.
Christopher Columbus, Letter to Sanchez (Latin), Basel 1493

15

Ferdinand, King of Spain.
Woodcut on the back cover of the first illustrated edition of the Columbus letter. The picture is not really a portrait but an all-purpose image of a Prince, who can be identified by the arms on the shield as well as the caption.

Christopher Columbus, Letter to Sanchez (Latin), Basel 1493

a prudent sailor who would not approach an unknown shore before dawn. He had the Salve sung and gave orders to "heave to" because, says the Journal, in all these islands there are "rocks under the sea close to land, and one must keep one's eyes open if one wishes to come to anchor . . . though the waters are very clear, and one can always see the bottom." With the first light of October 12, the squadron sailed round the south end of the island and found a passage through the coral reef to leeward. There, under a high sun, the Admiral and his Captains stepped onto the dazzling beach, and took ceremonial possession.

The Indians (meaning Asians) had watched the winged castles sail around the island. Now they timidly came out of the bush to touch the beards of the extra-terrestials, who seemed friendly. The Spaniards brought mirrors, red caps, and hawks' bells, which fascinated the Indians; they called them "chuc chuc." Their island they called "Guanahaní," but Columbus rechristened it San Salvador. These Indians, said he, "would more easily be converted to our Holy Faith by love than by force"; love at first sight in a paradise which, alas, would not outlive the first voyage; before the Barcelona Letter was done, the word "slaves" appeared. Columbus assured the Catholic Sovereigns that it would be applied only to idolaters, presumably Caribs, but in the end he found this pious promise impossible to keep.

III. THE LANDFALL CONTROVERSY AND THE INDIAN GUIDES

Columbus seems to have loved controversies: His birth, his religion, his geography, his seamanship, his first landfall, and his final resting place, all have proved controversial . . . unless perhaps it is historians who have made them so. I have tried to answer many of these questions, and I will now address the most persistent of all: Where did Columbus first set foot in the New World?

During at least two centuries after the discovery, no one worried very much about the identity of Guanahaní-San Salvador, the landfall island. Later, several islands in or near the Bahamas were proposed for the landfall. Today's San Salvador was for years known as Watling's, for some obscure British pirate, but in 1926 the British Government of the Bahamas considered the matter and renamed the island "San Salvador." In 1939–1940, Samuel Eliot Morison's famous Harvard Columbus Expedition confirmed the choice, and in 1964 he and I, documents in hand, reconfirmed it by flying low over the Bahamas, checking distances and directions, and photographing the details of the various islands. Since Morison's death, I have improved our findings while following Columbus' route in half a dozen square-riggers and yachts and in as many light planes flying high and low, and I know Sam would have approved; he never refused to face new evidence.

As far as I know, none of those who have disputed the San Salvador landfall has taken into account the directions Columbus received from his Indian guides; yet it is clear to me from the Journal that Columbus' guides must have taken him along the route they usually followed as they paddled their canoes from the landfall island to Cuba; what other route could they have proposed? In the letter Columbus says that on San Salvador he took ". . . some of these people by force . . . so that they might learn our language and give me news of what existed in those parts. And so it happened, for later they understood us and we them, either by speech or by signs: and they have been very useful to us. I am bringing them with me now . . ." We have seen how Columbus navigated on the high seas, but through the islands, from San Salvador on, it is obvious that all he could do

16

was indicate by gestures that he sought a great land where the Grand Khan had plenty of gold, then try to sail where his Indian guides pointed. In fact, if there had been no Indians, Columbus would never have found his way through the Bahamas to Cuba, Hispaniola, and home. The Indians were not just victims of the Discovery; they were indispensable participants, and to forget it is to underrate them.

The letter says that the Indians "travel all over those seas, it being a wonder to listen to the good accounts they give of everything . . . in all these islands there are very many canoes, similar to longboats, some of which are large and others smaller, many being even larger than a longboat of eighteen benches; but not as wide, for they are made of a single piece of timber. A longboat, however, could not keep up with them with oars alone, for they go with incredible speed. With these canoes they travel all over those islands, which are innumerable, and ply their merchandise. I have seen some of those canoes with 70 or 80 men aboard, and each with his oar." The Journal of October 13, 1492, adds that the Indians rowed with a paddle "such as a baker uses," and on October 26 it says that they had no sails; and Michele de Cuneo's account of October 15, 1495, confirms it. Surprising, because in a trade wind, raised paddles alone can move a canoe. The Indians may have been technologically primitive, but, as Columbus pointed out, they were no fools, and, wherever possible, they would have preferred paddling along a coast, "island-hopping" rather than facing the open sea, and never paddling aimlessly back and forth. On October 13, 17, 24, and 28 the Journal tells us that the Indians kept insisting that the land Columbus wanted lay roughly to the south or southwest, so they must have pointed in turn to each island where they would have rested while proceeding in that general direction.

Columbus' transatlantic course is certainly worth studying and following under sail, as Douglas Peck[1] has done, but the argument that, with modern corrections for leeway, drift, and perhaps magnetic variation, a plotted course leads to this or that island in the Bahamas is not valid. This argument is based on the assumption that Columbus simply noted his heading and his estimate of distance covered, without attempting to correct for currents, but we have seen that the Admiral did take currents into account, however approximately. Whether Columbus' corrections were accurate or not is beside the point: If one applies a modern correction to a course already corrected by Columbus, one compounds corrections, which automatically produces errors. And over a distance as long as Columbus' thirty-three-day transatlantic crossing, half a knot total error in drift would add up to three hundred and ninety-six nautical miles, which could place Columbus' landfall anywhere from Walker's Key, the northernmost point in the Bahamas, to Great Inagua, the southernmost.

Consequently, in order to identify the island of Columbus' first American landfall, we must follow a much shorter leg of the voyage than the Atlantic crossing: Columbus' course from his first landfall to the north coast of Cuba, via the intermediate islands which the Journal describes. Fortunately, changes in vegetation are relatively easy to take into account, and since the Bahamas are not subject to earthquakes, geologists tell us that, though sea level may have varied a few centimeters and hurricanes may have done damage, the islands' coastlines have probably not changed significantly.

Many of the islands once proposed as alternative landfalls to today's San Salvador have by now lost their

[1] "Recontruction of the Columbus Log from a Sailor-Navigator Viewpoint," Society for the History of Discovery, 1988.

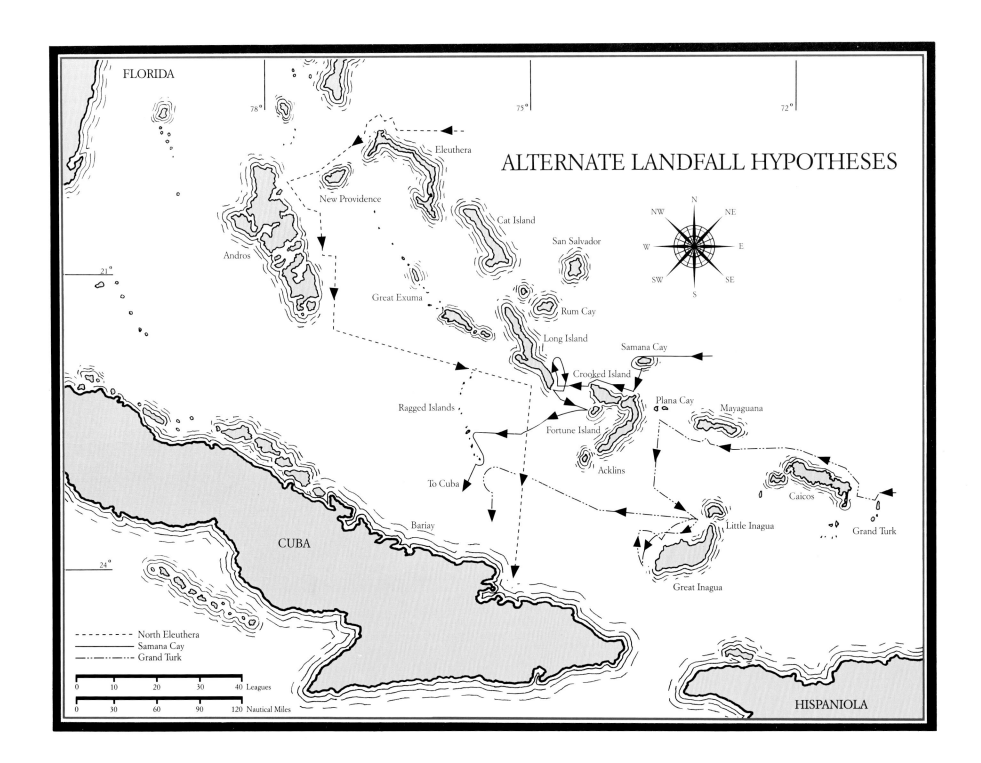

ALTERNATE LANDFALL HYPOTHESES

FLORIDA

78°
75°
72°

Eleuthera

New Providence

Cat Island

Andros

San Salvador

21°

Great Exuma

Rum Cay

Long Island

Samana Cay

Crooked Island

Plana Cay

Mayaguana

Ragged Islands

Fortune Island

Acklins

Caicos

To Cuba

Little Inagua

Grand Turk

Bariay

CUBA

24°

Great Inagua

HISPANIOLA

- - - - North Eleuthera
——— Samana Cay
—·—·— Grand Turk

```
0    10    20    30    40  Leagues
0    30    60    90   120  Nautical Miles
```

N
NW   NE
W   E
SW   SE
S

principal proponents. Three still have defenders: in the northern Bahamas, one of the islets adjacent to the north end of Eleuthera; in the south, Grand Turk Island; and in the mid-Bahamas, Samaná Cay. Let us examine these hypotheses with the same critera we will apply to San Salvador, and see if we can eliminate them.

The northern Bahamas hypothesis, proposed by Arne Molander, is attractive because it places the landfall closer to the latitude of the Canary island of Fierro. But Herrera, writing toward the end of the sixteenth century, says that Ponce de León, on his way from San Juan to Florida in 1513, stopped at San Salvador at latitude 25° 40′, which would place it halfway between the latitude of today's San Salvador and that of Fierro. Neil Sealey's paper on this subject is worth reading.[2] We have seen that magnetic variation explains why Columbus could have run somewhat south of west; and in any case the difference between San Salvador's latitude and Fierro's is equivalent only to a sighting over two knuckles held at arm's length, so that in an age of imprecise instruments, the latitude argument is not as weighty as it might seem. No island or combination of islands in the northern Bahamas fits the Journal's description of San Salvador, but the northern hypothesis does offer a good "Concepción," Providence Island. Unfortunately, from there on, Columbus would have had to sail to the northeastern coast of Andros Island ("Fernandina"), and then about one hundred and sixty-six nautical miles to the southwestern end of Long Island ("Isabela") in a night and a day (Journal, October 17 and 18, 1492), an average speed of about seven knots. This might be acceptable if Columbus had sailed this part of his course in a straight line, by day, and in good weather;

[2] "Ponce de León's Voyage in 1513 Points to San Salvador as Landfall of Columbus in 1492", *Encounter 92*, March 1989, Star Publishers Ltd., Nassau, Bahamas.

but the Journal tells us that he sailed at night, in heavy rain, and tacking downwind in order to stay away from an unknown shore, so a seven knot average is out of the question, and in any case southwestern Long Island makes a very poor Isabela. And if Columbus had landed in the northern Bahamas, would not the Indians have led him to Florida rather than all the way to Cuba?

The southern hypothesis was proposed by Martín Fernández de Navarrete in 1826, and Robert Power has now revived it. Its landfall island, Grand Turk, does have a lake in its center, but it is much too small for Guanahaní, which the Journal of October 13 describes as quite large ("*bien grande*"). And, this far south, the latitude problem really becomes accute. This hypothesis has to gum together several islands in order to form "Concepción," and in order to make the coast of Isabela run west it has to hypothesize to a point where all advantage is lost. Moreover, from Grand Turk, the Indians would surely have led Columbus directly to Cuba via Great Inagua, or, better still, straight down to Hispaniola, which lies only seventy-six nautical miles south of the southernmost cays of Turks-Caicos. The Indians were to lead Martín Alonso Pinzón down this route after he broke away from the fleet on the 20th of November, 1492. Why would they now lead Columbus all the way around to the northwest in order to get him to Cuba in the southwest?

Samaná Cay, which Gustavus Fox proposed for the landfall in 1882, a hypothesis Joseph Judge tried to revive in 1986, in no way fits the Journal's description of Guanahaní. It is about one-third the size of San Salvador; it cannot be seen from two leagues away (Journal, October 11); it runs east-west, so that when Columbus explored Guanahaní's coast to the northeast for most of a day, he would have run up on land; it bears no trace of a big central lake, in fact water is so scarce there that

Woodcut from a Vespucci letter showing a group of Indians talking while a butcher in the background prepares human limbs. The man urinating on the right is a reference to Vespucci's comment that though the Indians defecated in private they had no inhibitions about urination, even in the middle of a conversation.

[Amerigo Vespucci] Dis buchlin saget wie diezwe . . . van die Neuwen Welt (The Solderini Letter), Strasburg, 1509.

19

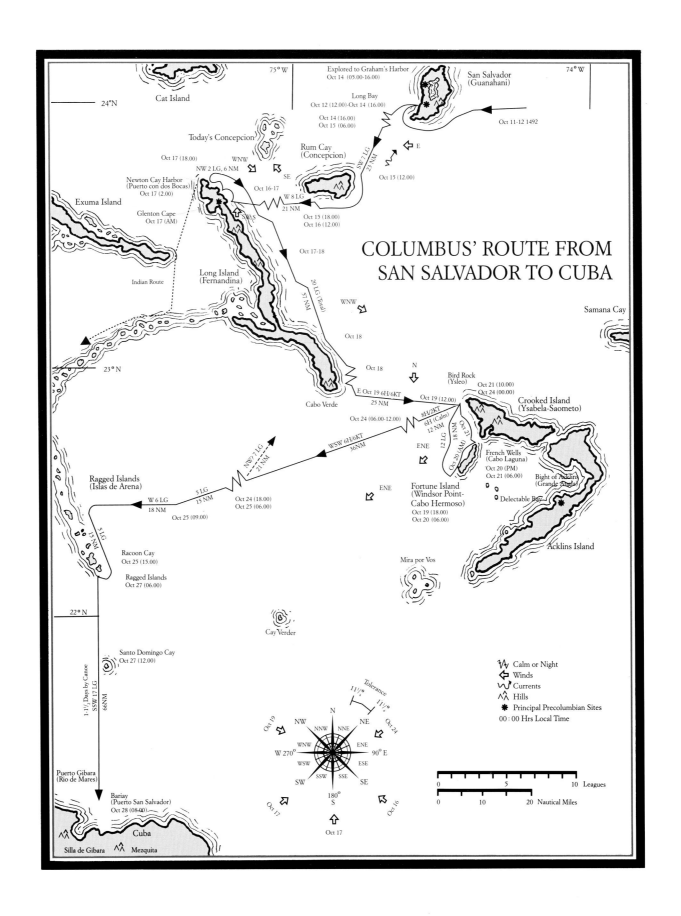

COLUMBUS' ROUTE FROM
SAN SALVADOR TO CUBA

Cat Island

San Salvador
(Guanahani)

Explored to Graham's Harbor
Oct 14 (05.00-16.00)

Long Bay
Oct 12 (12.00)-Oct 14 (16.00)

Oct 14 (16.00)
Oct 15 (06.00)

Oct 11-12 1492

24°N

75° W

74° W

Today's Concepcion

Rum Cay
(Concepcion)

Oct 17 (18.00)

WNW

NW 2 LG, 6 NM

SE

Oct 16-17

W 8 LG
21 NM

Oct 15 (12.00)

E

Newton Cay Harbor
(Puerto con dos Bocas)
Oct 17 (2.00)

Exuma Island

Glenton Cape
Oct 17 (AM)

SW 7 LG
23 NM

Oct 15 (18.00)
Oct 16 (12.00)

SW/S

Indian Route

Long Island
(Fernandina)

20 LG (Total)
57 NM

Oct 17-18

WNW

Oct 18

Samana Cay

23° N

Cabo Verde

Oct 18

N

E Oct 19 6H/6KT
25 NM

Bird Rock
(Ysleo)

Oct 21 (10.00)
Oct 24 (00.00)

Oct 19 (12.00)

Crooked Island
(Ysabela-Saometo)

8H/2KT
6H (Calm)
12 NM

Oct 24 (06.00-12.00)

12 LG

18 NM

ENE

Oct 21

French Wells
(Cabo Laguna)
Oct 20 (PM)
Oct 21 (06.00)

Bight of Acklins
(Grande Angla)

WSW 6H/6KT
36NM

NW 7 LG
2 NM

ENE

Fortune Island
(Windsor Point-
Cabo Hermoso)
Oct 19 (18.00)
Oct 20 (06.00)

Oct 20 (AM)

Delectable Bay

Ragged Islands
(Islas de Arena)

5 LG
15 NM

Oct 24 (18.00)
Oct 25 (06.00)

W 6 LG
18 NM

Oct 25 (09.00)

Acklins Island

15 NM
5 LG

Racoon Cay
Oct 25 (15.00)

Ragged Islands
Oct 27 (06.00)

Mira por Vos

22° N

Cay Verder

Santo Domingo Cay
Oct 27 (12.00)

1-1½ Days by Canoe
SSW 17 LG
66NM

Calm or Night

Winds

Currents

Hills

Principal Precolumbian Sites

00 : 00 Hrs Local Time

Puerto Gibara
(Rio de Mares)

Tolerance
11¼°
11¼°

Oct 19

NW

N

NE

Oct 24

Bariay
(Puerto San Salvador)
Oct 28 (08-40)

NNW

NNE

WNW

ENE

W 270°

90° E

WSW

ESE

Oct 17

SW

SSW

SSE

SE

Oct 16

Cuba

180°
S

Oct 17

0
5
10 Leagues

0
10
20 Nautical Miles

Silla de Gibara

Mezquita

the fishermen who come from Acklins Island do not settle in Samaná; its anchorage and its "great port" are so poor that I ran up on the corals trying to sail in; and it would take a bulldozer to separate its "peninsula" from the main island, whereas Columbus said it could easily be done by hand. On top of all this, the Samaná route's Concepción is composed of the north coasts of Acklins and Crooked Island unaccountably joined together, and its eastern coast does not face Samaná as it should (Journal, October 14), so Columbus could not have seen that it was five leagues long; and as they appear over the horizon, the hills of Acklins and Crooked look like fewer islands than those of Rum Cay on the San Salvador route.

On Columbus' second island, Fernandina, the Samaná route sends Columbus on a ten-nautical-mile voyage up and down the southeastern end of Long Island, much less than Columbus' twenty leagues (Journal, October 16, 1492), and it makes no sense to try to explain the difference by brazenly inserting the word "wind" in the Journal's entry of October 17, where Columbus simply says "It was scarce ('poco') and did not allow me to approach the land." The wind mentioned in the preceding sentence blew out of the west-northwest, so its being scarce could not have prevented Columbus from going ashore westwards; "*poco fondo*," as used on October 27, meaning "little depth" might be better. And this too-short exploration ends at Clarence Town where the coast turns briefly northwest in full view of the rest of Long Island, so how could Columbus have been trying to "sail around the island" that way (Journal, October 16 and 17)? As for Little Harbor, the Samaná route's "harbor with two mouths," its main entrance and the anchorage inside are deep enough for big yachts, whereas Columbus' harbor was too shallow for his fleet.

Next, having used Crooked Island for one-half of Concepción, the Samaná hypothesis must send Columbus back to Fortune Island, better known as Long Cay, a relatively small appendage of Crooked Island. This could hardly be the island Columbus named for the Queen, the Indians' great Saometo, the island of gold, larger even than Fernandina; and there is no break in it to separate Cabo Hermoso from Cabo de la Laguna. Worst of all, having sailed two continuous courses somewhat north of west, the Indians are now supposed to lead Columbus back east. Instead of this roundabout route, had Columbus first landed on Samaná, the Indians would surely have led him directly from Samaná to Cuba down the coast of Acklins to the Mira por Vos Cays, Cay Verde, and Cay Santo Domingo, much the shortest route for a canoe, and downwind. As to the Journal's statement of November 20, that Guanahaní lay eight leagues from Isabela, which might fit Samaná a little better than San Salvador, the fact is that Columbus, who had never sailed that course direct, made the estimate when he was already in Cuba, and Las Casas paraphrased this part of the Journal without quoting, then proceeded to make an obvious mess of headings and distances.

Finally, Samaná presents another kind of problem and it is an important one: In 1500, Juan de la Cosa, who was present with Columbus at the landfall as Master of the *Santa María*, drew the first map of America, which today hangs in the Naval Museum of Madrid, and is reproduced here on page 77. In this map he places two islands in approximately correct relationship and labels one "Guanahaní" and the other "Samaná," thus giving eyewitness testimony that the landfall island, Guanahaní, was different from Samaná. Moreover, in 1526, Alonso Chávez, in his *Espejo de Navegantes*, describes "Island number fifteen" as Samaná, and "Island number sixteen" as Guanahaní, which he specifically

A wild native woman swings at a well-dressed northern European burgher who has been distracted by three other attractive naked women. The composition is a novel rendering of the theme of the Judgment of Paris.

[Amerigo Vespucci] Dis buchlin saget wie diezwe . . . van die Neuwen Welt (The Solderini Letter), Strasburg, 1509.

identifies as the landfall. So Columbus' contemporaries and immediate successors were obviously sure that the first landfall did not occur on Samaná. Taviani has given many more cartographic instances to prove it.[3]

The Barcelona Letter pays little attention to the Bahamas, so, for the landfall, I will mostly navigate by the Journal, and the quotes I will use are my own free interpretations of Las Casas' text. We have seen that the original has never been found, and that the transcription we have was made by Las Casas, a friar, not a navigator, who tells us he worked from a copy, not from the original; he also paraphrased a great deal and says so, and he altered his text nine hundred and forty-eight times, seventy-eight times directly affecting leagues, miles, or sailing directions. Moreover, the Journal is difficult to read because it jumps back and forth in time and mixes navigational information with descriptions. Consequently, as we navigate by the Journal, we must always check it either against other parts of the Journal itself, or against other documents. And if differences remain, I submit that we should accept the information given last. The Journal does tell us many times (October 25, 27, etc.) that the fleet's usual fair-weather speed through the islands was two leagues per hour, equivalent to some six knots, a reasonable speed.

Taking all this into account, let us set sail from San Salvador for Cuba at about six knots (less, of course, where Columbus sailed in bad weather or at night), and without forgetting this key question: Is this the route an Indian would usually have chosen in order to paddle southwest to Cuba? Readers who do not care to sail, not even vicariously, can profitably skip the next chapter, but those who wish to come along will see that the route

from San Salvador to Cuba is the only one which fits the sailing directions Columbus left us.

IV. The Bahamas

Island I: Guanahaní (San Salvador)

At ten P.M. on Thursday, October 11, 1492, Columbus saw a light, and on Friday at two A.M. Rodrigo de Triana cried *"Tierra!"* ("Land ho!"). Ruth Wolper,[1] the doyenne of San Salvador, has given the best explanation of the light: Natives of today's San Salvador still build fires on the bluffs in order to fend off sand flies and mosquitoes. But it has been argued that, because of the four hours which passed between the sighting of the light and the landfall, the light must have been on a different island than San Salvador. The Journal of October 11 says that the fleet covered more than sixty-five nautical miles from nightfall to two A.M. on the 12th, when the landfall occurred, which would mean that at ten P.M. Columbus was almost thirty-four nautical miles away from the landfall, plus two nautical miles from landfall to land (Journal, October 14), too far for Columbus to have seen the light. I cannot accept the two-island hypothesis, for in those circumstances, who would sail past an island with a light on it to seek another, unseen island? So I propose that Columbus may have seen the reflection of the Indians' fires on a cloud and sailed toward it.

On October 14, Columbus points out that reefs surround all these islands, and the fact is that they are much more dangerous along their eastern coasts. San Salvador's is studded with modern wrecks right under the old monument on the eastern side of the island;

[3] "Why We Are Favorable for the Watling-San Salvador Landfall," *Columbus and His World*, Bahamian Field Station, Ft. Lauderdale, Florida.

[1] "A New Theory Identifying Columbus' Light." Smithsonian Miscellaneous Collections, Volume 148 No. 1, Sept. 11, 1964.

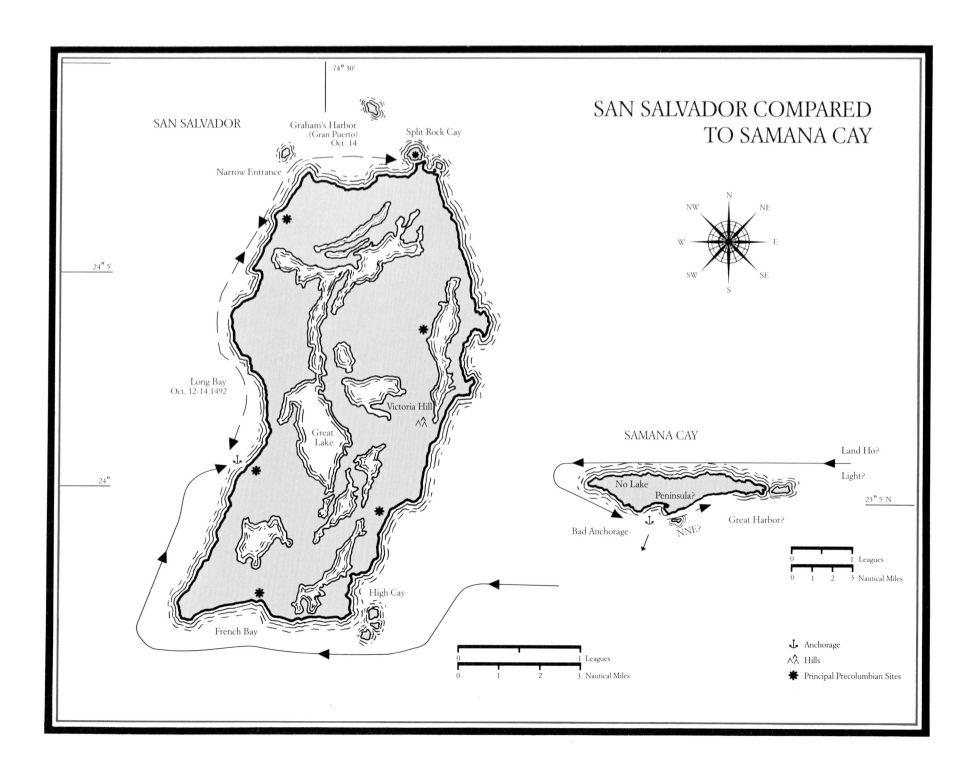

SAN SALVADOR COMPARED
TO SAMANA CAY

SAN SALVADOR

74° 30'

Graham's Harbor
(Gran Puerto)
Oct. 14

Split Rock Cay

Narrow Entrance

N
NW   NE

W   E

SW   SE

S

24° 5'

Long Bay
Oct. 12-14 1492

Victoria Hill

Great
Lake

SAMANA CAY

Land Ho?

24°

Light?

No Lake

23° 5' N

Peninsula?

Bad Anchorage

Great Harbor?

NNE?

0   1 Leagues

0   1   2   3 Nautical Miles

High Cay

French Bay

0   1 Leagues

0   1   2   3 Nautical Miles

⚓ Anchorage

⋀⋀ Hills

✳ Principal Precolumbian Sites

23

beaches suitable for landing face west. I sailed in from the east before dawn and saw San Salvador's white sandstone bluffs shining in the moonlight. Then I rounded South End and sailed carefully up the west coast until I saw a break in the coral, just as Columbus must have done. Ruth Wolper had a cross put up at Long Bay, which bears Morison's name and mine: surely the right spot, because it is near the first break in the reef, and because archaeology and geology also help with the identification, though they cannot prove it: Only a few steps from our cross, Charles Hoffman[2] has found glass beads and other objects of Spanish origin in conjunction with Indian sherds, something which has not turned up on any other Bahamian island. And the "beach-rock" which Columbus described (January 5, 1493) as the natural building blocks he saw on Guanahaní, forms on these beaches by diagenesis. I have stubbed my toe on a square block near Long Bay. According to the Journal, Guanahaní-San Salvador was flat, with green trees, many waters, and a large lagoon in the center: Today's San Salvador has many bodies of water (*guana* to the Indians, as in "Guanahaní") and a large lagoon in the center. By European standards, it is flat, and it is green, and John Winter[3] has found stumps of great trees, which American loyalists cut down when they moved to the Bahamas during the Revolution.

At dawn on Sunday, October 14, Columbus and his men set out in the nao's barge *(batel)* and the caravels' gigs *(barcas)*, "to explore the island . . . to the north-northeast . . . to see the other side which is to the east," more proof that the expedition had landed on the western shore and had seen the southern end of the island as they sailed around it. On the way, they saw several villages from which Indians came to offer food and water to the visitors from heaven. Inside a narrow entrance through the reef, they found a huge harbor, where "the sea moves no more than in a well" (Journal, October 14). It was protected by a peninsula which the Journal says could be made into an island in three days, on which stood three houses. On today's San Salvador, the entrance to Graham's Harbor through the reef is indeed narrow, and the southeastern end of the harbor is usually calm enough. The tide periodically makes an island out of Split Cay, a peninsula on which precolumbian remains have been found. Columbus does not say that his men rowed all the way along the shore of San Salvador, and the nao's barge may well have carried a lateen sail, but in any case to row north-northeast from Long Bay to Graham's Harbor and back between first light (five A.M.) and midafternoon is no problem; Maxwell Stephen Ferguson rowed the course one way on October 28, 1986, in three hours and twenty minutes. Columbus says that some of the Indians who came down to the beach wore gold ornaments which they indicated came from the southwest. He thought the gold must be from Cipango (Japan), so he decided to sail southwest as soon as possible. On the afternoon of Sunday, October 14, he and his men returned to the ships and raised anchors.

Island II: Concepción (Rum Cay)

From Guanahaní Columbus headed for the largest of the "many islands" he saw to the southwest. The current ran against the fleet, and since it was too late to reach the next island in daylight, they hove to for the night. On Monday, October 15, starting at dawn, they completed the seven leagues southwest to the island which Columbus named Santa María de la Concepción. At midday they saw its east coast, five leagues long and

[2] "Archaeological Investigations at the Long Bay Site, San Salvador, Bahamas," Columbus and His World, Bahamian Field Station, Ft. Lauderdale, Florida.
[3] "San Salvador in 1492: Its Geography and Ecology", Columbus and His World, Bahamian Field Station, FT. Lauderdale, FLA.

facing Guanahaní, then they sailed along the south coast, ten leagues long or more. At sunset they anchored near the southwest end of the island and spent the night on board.

Rum Cay lies twenty-three nautical miles to the southwest of San Salvador, and its best anchorage is under its south shore. But why did Columbus weigh anchors from San Salvador in the afternoon? Because from mast height he could just see two of the hills of the next island. I have seen them on the horizon from high ground on South End, San Salvador, and I think this is the first instance of the influence of the Indian guides, who surely pointed them out. As to the "many islands," the Journal does not say that Columbus saw them as soon as he sailed, and he may well be referring to the many Bahamas he eventually saw; in fact, on October 14, he goes on to describe islands he has not yet visited. But in any case, as one sails toward Rum Cay, hill after hill begins to appear above the horizon until they look like eight separate islands. And, as Don Gerace, Director of the Field Station on San Salvador island, has pointed out, if one stays to the north, one can also see today's "Concepción"; and later Long Island's hills, too. Instead of five by ten leagues Rum Cay measures five by ten Roman miles, so I suggest that Las Casas confused leagues with miles, just as he did on January 22, 1493, when he said the fleet made six leagues per hour, an impossible speed unless we read "miles" instead of "leagues." On October 11 and 27 he made the same mistake, then corrected it. And why did it take Columbus so long to reach his anchorage in the southwest of Concepción? Because, as he says, he started with an adverse current, then took the time to have a good look at both the east and the south coasts of Concepción.

Early on Tuesday the 16th, Columbus and his men went ashore in armed longboats. One of the Indian "interpreters" escaped in a canoe, and another Indian approached carrying a ball of cotton. Columbus gave him a red cap, bangles of green glass beads, and hawk's-bell earrings, then set him free; he realized he would need friends. Late in the morning of Tuesday, October 16, the wind made up from the southeast, which made the anchorage unsafe for Columbus, as it did for me. So the fleet left Concepción and sailed eight leagues west to a cape on the east coast of the next island, which Columbus called Fernandina.

Island III: Fernandina (Long Island)

Long Island's Glenton Cape is visible shortly after one sails west from Rum Cay, twenty-one nautical miles to the west, and the Indian guides knew it. They also knew that Long Island ran far to the south, and Columbus confirms that Fernandina's coast ran more than twenty leagues northwest-southeast. Long Island runs fifty-seven nautical miles northwest-southeast, an almost perfect fit. Halfway across, another solitary Indian in a canoe turned up. He carried not only cassava bread, water, and dry leaves (tobacco?), but also glass beads and two Spanish coins. He must have paddled all the way from San Salvador, says the Journal, via Concepción; which supports my argument that his Indian guides must have been leading Columbus along their usual canoe route. He was given bread and honey "so that he may speak well of us," and the fleet spent the night becalmed outside Fernandina's reef. On Wednesday, October 17, during the second half of the morning, Columbus sent the barge ashore for water, which is still available from wells not far from some precolumbian remains behind Glenton Cape.

At midday, with the wind out of the south and southwest, the fleet followed the coast of Fernandina two leagues to the northwest "toward the end of the island." Near the cape, they found a large, shallow port with two entrances, and what looked like a river mouth. While

European sailors, dressed as prosperous Northern European townsmen, trying to attract the suspicious natives with gifts.

[Amerigo Vespucci] Dis buchlin saget wie diezwe . . . van die Neuwen Welt (The Solderini Letter), Strasburg, 1509.

The earliest attempts at accurate drawings of American subjects appeared long after Columbus. In this depiction of Indian agriculture, note the palm trees among the conventional European foliage. Gonzalo Fernando de Oviedo y Valdés, La Historia General de Las Indias, Seville, 1535.

the boats went in for more water, Columbus walked about for two hours, marveling at the trees, the birds, the fish, and a dog that wore a gold ring in its nose. Here the older ("married") women wore cotton panties (*bragas*); one wonders where they learned their modesty. Their houses were clean and had high "chimneys," presumably steep roofs. Their beds were like cotton nets: the first mention of the hammock, which sailors would soon adopt. It has been asked why Columbus should have kept looking for water after apparently obtaining plenty on San Salvador. The fact is that sailors are always interested in three things: water, verdure, and women. Next, the fleet sailed northwest to where the coast began to run east-west. On October 16 and 17, Columbus says he intended to sail around the island that way, obviously planning to continue down the lee of the island, toward the south and southeast where, the Indians insisted, lay the island of gold. But the wind veered to the west-northwest, so he decided instead to sail all night along the eastern coast of Fernandina, "sometimes east, sometimes southeast," in order to stay away from the reefs. It rained hard all night. On the night of the 18th the fleet lay to, probably off the cape which Columbus later christened Cabo Verde.

I have stood off, as Columbus did, outside a good but shallow port with two mouths, Newton Cay Harbor, six nautical miles (two leagues) northwest of Glenton Cape. It is near Seymour's, a village which still draws water from several old wells, and which is surrounded by trees filled with the song of the mockingbird. What looks like a river, though it carries salt water, empties into the harbor; today it is spanned by a small bridge. The Journal's "*surgir*" has often been translated as "to anchor," so it has been argued that one cannot anchor outside Newton Cay Harbor, but the fact is that on Monday the 15th Columbus pointed out that along these islands the bottom is too deep to reach; and *surgir* does not nec-

essarily mean "to anchor." García de Palacio, in his *Instrucción Náutica* of 1587, says that *surgir* means simply to call at a port (*hacer escala* or *tomar puerto*). And later, on August 19, 1498, the Journal of the third voyage uses *surgir* for Columbus' arrival half-way between the islands of Alta Vela and Beata in the south of Hispaniola, where it is far too deep to anchor.

From Newton Cay Harbor and following the coast to the north-northwest, one reaches a point where it turns sharply west and then south. This is not exactly east-west as the Journal says on October 17, 1492, but, because of the change of wind, Columbus never followed this coast, so it is obvious that he merely surmised that after turning west it must have run east-west. The original idea of sailing around the north end of the island makes a great deal of sense; the Indians knew that this was the way to pick up the Ragged Island chain and follow it all the way to the point nearest to Cuba. And when the wind veered to west-northwest it again makes sense that Columbus should have decided that the only thing to do was to sail southeast all night and all day along the east coast of Long Island, tacking downwind in order to stay in deep water. Columbus surely reduced speed at night, perhaps to two or three knots, so twenty-four hours fits the length of Long Island.

Island IV: Isabela (Crooked Island)

Once the original plan of sailing around the north end of Long Island and down the Raggeds had been abandoned, the Indians obviously decided to try to satisfy Columbus with Saomet, the island of gold, "larger even than Fernandina," so that he would let them go home. On Friday, October 19, the fleet sailed east from Cape Verde at dawn. The ships fanned out and then rejoined, in order not to miss Saomet, and before midday the fleet arrived at a cape where there was an "*Ysleo*," which, according to Las Casas, means a small island. It was protected by reefs and stood at the north end of Saomet, which was indeed large and had high hills. Columbus renamed it Isabela. Today's Bird Rock stands at the northwestern extreme of Crooked Island, and it is well protected by reefs, just as Columbus' *Ysleo* was. It lies twenty-five nautical miles east of Long Island, a reasonable distance for the fleet to have covered between dawn and noon, considering that the ships separated and then came together again, and that they were not sailing with the prevailing wind. Crooked Island corresponds well with the Journal's description of Isabela; it is large, has plenty of water, and its hills are over one hundred and fifty feet high, some of the highest in the Bahamas.

Next Columbus says he sailed with a north wind along a coast which ran "twelve leagues west" to Cabo Hermoso, which the fleet reached in the evening; but on Saturday, October 20, he says he decided to return whence he had come, to the north-northwest "to try and round the island that way," so the coast must have run north-south not east-west. In fact if it had run west, Columbus would have bumped into it when he first approached the *Ysleo* from the east. Las Casas crossed out "west" then wrote it in again, so he seems to have suspected that he was about to make another of his navigational mistakes. Columbus followed this coast down to Cabo Hermoso. The coast was lined with beaches, and on October 19 the Journal says that the part of it on which the cape stood was separated from Isabela by a small cay. To the northeast of the cape lay a great bay across which, according to the Indians, lived the King of Saomet. Columbus tried to sail into it, but found it too shallow.

Fortune Island (also known as Long Cay) is separated from Crooked by one big cay and two small ones, and Windsor Point, its southern extreme, is sandy to the north and solid rock to the south, just as Columbus describes Cabo Hermoso. Why *"hermoso,"* which means beautiful? Not only because it was green, but also because an anchorage is beautiful for a sailor when the bottom is clean all around. I have spent a pleasant night there, riding quietly at anchor. Across the shallow Bight of Acklins, where the King of Saomet was supposed to live, a large concentration of precolumbian remains has been found at Delectable Bay. But, as the Journal points out, the bight is in fact too shallow to enter.

On Saturday, October 20, at dawn, the fleet was back at Cabo de la Laguna at the southwest end of Saomet. Again Columbus tried to sail northeast and east, but once more it was too shallow. Today's French Wells lies on the southern extreme of Crooked Island, on the way back from Windsor Point to Bird Rock. Behind a dazzling beach, Turtle Creek brings fresh water from Turtle Sound, which explains the name Cabo de la Laguna. And again the bight is too shallow to enter. The wind was light, and Columbus decided to return to the *Ysleo*.

Columbus arrived back at Cabo del Ysleo on Sunday, October 21, at ten A.M., and stayed there four days, waiting for the "King," who never turned up. I suggest Columbus must have established his base, as we did, off Landrail Point on Crooked Island, just south of Bird Rock. He explored the island and found a large lagoon (Turtle Sound) but only one house. Here, says Columbus, the trees and the grass were as green as in Andalusia in spring, and the men killed an iguana, seven palms long, and dried its skin to bring to the Sovereigns. On Monday, October 22, many Indians appeared. They brought water, and spoke of a great island called Colba which Columbus thought might finally be Cipangu, and of another great island beyond, which they called Bohío. On Tuesday, October 23, the wind was calm and it rained, "but it was not cold." Finally, on Wednesday, October 24, Columbus weighed anchors at midnight for

Colba (Cuba), which the Indians insisted lay to the west-southwest.

Island V: Islas de Arena (Ragged Islands)

Since Saomet-Isabela had not satisfied Columbus, the Indian guides evidently decided they had better get back on the Ragged Island route to Cuba, the route they had failed to pick up from northern Long Island because of the change of wind. From midnight to dawn on October 24 the fleet sailed west-southwest in rain, with light and variable winds, then lay becalmed until midday when a "loving" wind made up. They hoisted all sails and held the same heading with the wind freshening, and as darkness fell, they reached a point where Columbus estimated that Cape Verde lay seven leagues to the northwest. The distance is right, but the direction should be northeast; not surprising, since Las Casas sometimes confused directions, for example, on October 16 and 17, when he first described Fernandina as running northwest-southsouthwest, then northnorthwest-southsoutheast. In any case, this "fix," estimated by Columbus in the dusk, can be placed anywhere between Isabela and the Islas de Arena without affecting the rest of the course. The wind became heavy, then it rained, so the fleet shortened sail and lay to at night in the rain, hardly moving at all in order to avoid running onto any hidden reefs. On Thursday, October 25, from dawn to three P.M., they sailed eleven leagues, first west-southwest, then west. Finally they saw seven or eight islands which ran north-south, and sailed another five leagues to find an anchorage to the south. On Friday, October 26, they rested south of the islands, which Columbus called Islas de Arena, the Sandy, or Ragged, Islands.

Six hours with a light, variable wind during the night of October 23–24, at perhaps two knots, then calm, then six hours at six knots, then another thirty-three nautical miles on October 25, brings Columbus' two-day total to eighty-one nautical miles west-southwest; and the actual course from Crooked Island to the Ragged Islands is eighty-five nautical miles somewhat north of west-southwest.

The identification of the sandy Ragged Islands with Islas de Arena is not seriously disputed. But why did Columbus sail from Isabela at midnight? The Journal of October 24 suggests the answer: It says Columbus was beginning to understand the Indians' sign language, so they probably got it across to him that the next leg was the longest of the voyage, and that he had better get under way as soon as the wind allowed it. In our case, we overslept and sailed shortly before dawn, and we soon found out that we could not reach the Ragged Islands in daylight. So, after fourteen hours sailing, we had to jog off for another ten hours waiting for the dawn. Not a pleasant experience in ten-foot waves and a thirty-mile wind, probably rather like the conditions that made Columbus shorten sail. Finally, at dawn we had to move fifteen nautical miles (five leagues) to the south end of the islands and around, to find a good anchorage and a well-earned rest, just like Columbus.

Island VI: Juana (Cuba)

On Saturday, October 27, at dawn, the Journal says that Columbus sailed seventeen leagues south-southwest from the Islas de Arena. Before nightfall he saw land, and lay to for the night. Cuba was still too distant, so Columbus must have seen small Cay Santo Domingo, to which the Indian guides surely pointed. We stood off there very uncomfortably, so for Columbus' ships it could have offered no shelter. The Indians had told him that they normally paddled from Islas de Arena to Cuba in a day and a half; once more, our Indian canoe route. On November 14, the Journal says the canoes covered seven leagues during a whole day, an average speed of something less than two knots, and from the Ragged Islands to Cuba the Indians would have had to paddle day and night, so a day and a half would mean thirty-six hours, which at something less than two knots would fit the total distance of seventy-two nautical miles. Finally, on Sunday, October 28, Columbus completed his voyage south-southwest to Cuba, which he baptized Juana.

Once in Cuba, the fleet entered a "river mouth" twelve fathoms deep, and anchored inside with plenty of room to tack. Columbus went up the river in his longboat, and on Monday, October 29, he says that the river mouth was salt. He saw many palm trees, different from the ones he knew, with fronds so big that they served to roof the Indian houses: Royal Palm. Inland stood beautiful mountains, as high as La Peña de los Enamorados near Granada, and one of them had another small hill on top which looked like a mosque. This hill, mosque and all, stands behind Bahía Bariay, Cuba, and sailors now call it *"La Teta de Bariay."* Not far to the west, Columbus came upon a much bigger port which he called Rio de Mares. In the background stood two round hills, today known as "The Saddle." They stand behind Puerto Gibara, which certainly deserves the name *"mares"*; it is so large that inside it my dinghy was swamped by waves.

Columbus said that the blessed smell of flowers and trees and earth across the water was the sweetest thing in the world. It is. As we approached Cuba before daylight, it was my turn at the tiller, and the changing breeze brought me the fragrance of the land. As the dawn sketched out the shore, I saw to starboard the two round hills, and to port, the mountain with a mosque on top. Cipango!

V. Cuba, Hispaniola, and Home

As soon as they saw the fleet approaching, the Cuban Indians fled. Columbus says that they cultivated cinna-mon, beans, some kind of nuts, and *"ñames,"* sweet potatoes which "looked like carrots but tasted like chestnuts." In their houses, he found fishing tackle and dogs that did not bark, and for the first time, "many statues shaped like women." These statues are still called *Cemíes,* and Columbus wondered whether they were ornaments or idols, but concluded that the Indians were not idolaters, for "they immediately repeat our prayers, and make the Sign of the Cross." Poor Indians! They were eager to please, and would mimic almost anything.

Columbus, hopefully, sent an embassy to the nearest big settlement to seek news of the Grand Khan. It included Luis de Torres, the interpreter, who spoke Hebrew and Arabic, and Rodrigo de Jeréz who had once visited an African king. They had a great time, probably at Chorro de Maita, where Cuban archaeologist José Manuel Guarch showed me a large Taíno cemetery. But instead of gold and spices, they brought back "fire-brands" of herbs that gave off a pleasant smoke which the Indians inhaled through the nose; it was tobacco, which was to prove even more addictive than gold. On October 30 and 31, Columbus sailed west from Gibara to today's Punta Malagueta or thereabouts. He found nothing of interest, and when the coast trended increasingly to the north, he came about and returned to Gibara, where he spent two weeks. He took on six more Indian men, three children, and seven women "to keep the Indians happy and to teach our men their language"; probably the beginning of a fruitful blending of races and languages. With these new passengers, a total of twenty Indians went to Spain after the first voyage, six Bahamians, and fourteen Cubans (two got away on November 17).

Sailing along the Cuban coast to the east, on November 12 Columbus rounded Cabo de Cuba, today's Cabo Lucrecia, and, bypassing Bahía de Nipe, he entered

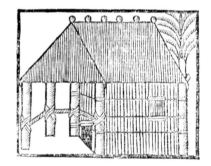

Fairly accurate rendering of a native house ("bohío") in Hispaniola.

Gonzalo Fernando de Oviedo y Valdés, La Historia General de Las Indias, Seville, 1535.

Bahía Tánamo, which he called El Mar de Nuestra Señora. It is an inland sea graced with many islands, and its mouth is so narrow that without radar we would have had a hard time finding it, so the Indians must have found it for Columbus. Inside there are many good anchorages, including one to port as one enters, where we anchored, which Columbus called Puerto Príncipe. There, on November 11 he mentions *"nueces grandes de la India,"* which some have understood to mean coconuts, but which were probably *Chrysobalanus icaco,* since the coconut palm had not yet arrived in the Caribbean. He also mentions a large rat, the Hutía, which is still bred in Cuba as a delicacy. The Indians told Columbus that to the east, gold could be picked up on the beach of "Baneque," today's Great Inagua, which produces nothing but salt. Columbus decided to try to reach it, but he never made it against the wind, and during his third abortive attempt, Martín Alonso Pinzón went off on his own in the faster *Pinta*; "This and much more has he done to me," wrote the Admiral, and turned back to Cuba.

As the fleet proceeded eastward along the coast, the Indian guides became more and more terrified of running into Caribs, until they could hardly speak, but Columbus thought they exaggerated. Perhaps, says he, the Caribs were not really cannibals; they simply never gave back their prisoners. After all, if they had arms, they must be rational. Good Renaissance reasoning.

On November 24, Columbus found a good harbor behind a flat island which he called Santa Catalina, today's Puerto Moa. Here, for the first time, he picked up stones in the river which seemed to be studded with gold and other metals, and Puerto Moa is still an important mining center. He also noted beautiful stands of spruce, for cutting ship's masts. On the 26th he passed Punta Gorda, a prominent headland which he called Cabo Pico, and beyond the next headland, which still bears the name he gave it, Cabo Campana, he came to today's Baracoa, a harbor "round as a soup bowl." He called it Puerto Santo, surely in memory of the island near Madeira where he had spent his first married years with Felipa. Here the Indians were really numerous and had plenty of good houses, cultivated fields, and enormous canoes which they built under roofs, as they are still built in Baracoa under thatch. As usual, first the Indians fled, then they returned because they were curious, and finally they became friendly.

But on December 3 something new occurred: the Baracoans staged a big demonstration headed by a plumed cacique who made a speech. At first Columbus thought he was being welcomed, but when he saw that his interpreters were trembling, he knew he was being asked to leave. A demonstration with a crossbow changed all that, but at least the Indians had tried! Presents were soon exchanged, and Columbus settled down, thanking God that thus far no one on board had been ill, "not even with a headache." He erected a cross, and what remains of it is still in the church; I helped the parish priest carry it to its original location at the mouth of the harbor. A less pious note was a human head which Columbus saw hanging in a basket; he guessed that it was just the memento of an ancestor, which it probably was, since the Taínos were never headhunters.

Finally, on December 4, Columbus reached the eastern end of Cuba at Cabo Lindo, today's Punta del Fraile, seven leagues north of Cape Maisi, which, says Bernaldez, Columbus later named Cape Alpha and Omega, the beginning and the end of Asia. To the east must lie Cipango. Impatiently, *Santa María* and *Niña* crossed the eighteen leagues which the Barcelona Letter rightly says separate Cuba from Hispaniola; not an easy crossing, I can attest. On Saint Nicholas' Day, December 6, they entered the magnificent natural port which still bears the Saint's name, then followed the coast to the northeast, rounded Cape Cinquín, and on December 7 established a base in Puerto Concepción, today's Moustique. Once again Columbus heard mention of the Caribs and their island, Caniba, which he immediately identified with the land of the *"Gran Can."* In Concepción, on December 17, a cacique showed Columbus a piece of gold leaf as big as his hand, but insisted on selling it bit by bit, and when it was finished, he said he would send for more. Pretty clever this Indian, says Columbus. Then he spent two hard weeks bucking wind and current through Tortuga Channel; I have tried to make headway against those winds and seas, and do not recommend it.

At last out of the channel, Columbus noted a cape which looks like a sleeping elephant, *"Cabo Elefante,"* today's Grande Pointe. Then he rounded today's Pointe Limbé, which he called Cabo Alto y Bajo, and on December 20 entered El Mar de Santo Tomé, behind Isla Amiga. There his sailors had a great time with the local ladies, a tradition which lasted for many years and gave the harbor its modern name, Acul ("Welcome") Bay. It is a beautiful bay into which we sailed through the reefs by following Columbus' instructions and passing between Isla Amiga and the western headland. Inside, says Columbus, it is so still that one can rely on any old anchor-line; true in today's mirror-quiet Lombard Cove. The Indian interpreters and the Spaniards were beginning to understand each other, but when the Indians pointed to the next *"bohío,"* their name for a house, Columbus understood that *bohío* was the Indian name for the island, which he still hoped was Cipango, an impression which was confirmed when the Indians mentioned "Cibao," the fertile heartland of Bohío-Hispaniola. Wishful thinking and similar names are a heady mixture.

The Journal of December 23 says that during the next few days a thousand Indians paraded through the flagship, including several chiefs who behaved with great dignity; they had good manners and did not waste any words, which confirmed Columbus in his policy of treating them kindly. Among them, Guacanagarí stood out; he was cacique of the whole of Marién, the western part of north Hispaniola, and gave Columbus a belt adorned with a mask trimmed with gold. Columbus gave him a pair of gloves with which, to the delight of his people, Guacanagarí paraded up and down the beach. On the 22nd, Columbus had noted how innocent the Indians were, and how greedy the Spaniards. Guacanagarí invited the Admiral to visit his "capital," and at dawn on December 23 Columbus sent the longboats east to scout the way with the cacique's guides. They returned at nightfall, reporting that Guacanagarí's village was a very large one which lay nearly three leagues to the southeast of the next cape, Punta Santa, today's Pointe Picolet at the entrance of Cap Haitien, and that reefs ran all the way there. But "they had seen where one could pass" (so had we, but we crashed into a reef marker anyhow!).

At dawn on December 24th, *Santa María* and *Niña* set out along the chosen route, with a gentle land breeze, the *"Terral,"* which, as the Journal tells us repeatedly, blows at night. At eleven o'clock, the fleet was becalmed, so after two nights of festivity, Columbus went below in the flagship to get some rest. Its Master, Juan de la Cosa, whose watch it was, also fell asleep, leaving a ship's boy in charge, a practice the Admiral had expressly forbidden. Hangovers can be blamed for many historic events. *"Mansamente"* (softly), says the Journal, the current nudged *Santa María* onto a reef, and at midnight the ship's boy felt the tiller tremble, then freeze (I know the feeling). He gave the alarm, and Columbus rushed on deck and sent Juan de la Cosa out in the longboat to set a stern anchor so the capstan

A dug-out canoe such as those mentioned in the Barcelona Letter.
Gonzalo Fernando de Oviedo y Valdés, La Historia General de Las Indias, Seville, 1535.

could be used to kedge *Santa María* free. Instead, La Cosa rowed to *Niña,* presumably to seek help, and while he returned, the flagship went firmly aground, broadside to the rising swell which soon began to drop her on the bottom until her seams split. Columbus decided to fell her mast to reduce weight, then went with his men to the caravel which had anchored half a league to windward. Once again, I imagine, he got very little sleep.

As Christmas day dawned, Columbus returned to the nao, which he had resolved to abandon, not an easy decision for a newly promoted Admiral. He sent for help to Guacanagarí's village which lay one league and a half beyond the wreck, and decided to build a fort with a moat *("cava")* which he named Navidad. Some have understood that *Santa María's* timbers were used to build the fort, but the Journal says *Santa María* remained "intact," except for a cannon shot through its side. Today, on Cay Brulé, a slightly raised peninsula near Bord de Mer de Limonade, a sandy little village on the beach, stand the remains of a French fort, probably on the location of Navidad, for it is a good place for a fort. As for *Santa María*, I think it is to be found on the western extreme of the barrier reef.

Guacanagarí wept at the Admiral's plight, and provided his best canoes so that everything that could be salvaged from *Santa María* could be brought to his village and stored. Nevertheless, to make sure that his loyalty would not waver, Columbus ordered an artillery demonstration against the grounded nao, and the men staged a war game. The cacique kept insisting that Columbus should stay; he had probably arranged with the neighboring caciques that "all gold should pass through his hands" says the Journal. In the Barcelona Letter Columbus says, "I have great friendship with the king of that land . . . But even if he were to change his mind and act against my men, neither he nor his people know anything about weapons, and go around naked, as I

have said: they are the most faint-hearted people in the world, and the few men I have left behind would suffice to destroy the whole of that land. The island offers no danger to their lives as long as they know how to govern it."

In the Journal of December 26, Columbus raved against La Cosa for having left a boy in charge of *Santa María,* and against the town of Palos for having provided him with a ship "too heavy for discovery," and on December 31 against Martín Alonso Pinzón for having abandoned him. But, typically, he found consolation in the thought that the site of Navidad, which at first he had not liked, might be "providential," which he confirms in the letter. Now he turned his attention to the problem of getting home with the news of his discovery, and preventing Pinzón from getting there first "and telling lies." Spain was no more than a month's sail from Navidad, and the Admiral, whose imagination always ran ahead, was already planning to return to Hispaniola with everything needed to establish a real colony. A farewell ceremony was performed with Guacanagarí, who placed his crown on Columbus' head and received a purple cloak, and on January 2 *Niña* sailed east after leaving the bay "through a broader channel to the northwest." At Montecristi, between a small island and the mountain, Columbus found a good port and noted that Montecristi was a good landmark for finding Navidad because "it is shaped like a huge tent."

The Indians had told Columbus that they had seen *Pinta,* and as he sailed east on January 6, Columbus met her, ten leagues east of Navidad. Grudgingly, he pardoned Pinzón, who had been away for all of a month and a half; he brought gold from the Yaque del Norte River, where Columbus later saw gold dust stick to his water casks. Together, the two caravels returned to Montecristi's good harbor, then on January 9, heading east, they passed Punta Roja, where Columbus saw three "sirens," probably manatees, and remarked that they were not as beautiful as they were cracked up to be. On January 10 the two caravels stopped at Rio de Gracia, probably today's Estero Hondo, surely called Gracia because of the pardon Columbus had granted Pinzón, who had spent sixteen days there "pocketing half the gold" while worms devoured *Pinta's* bottom. Pressing on, they passed Belprado, probably Cape Isabela, where Columbus would establish the ill-fated capital of his second voyage; and lofty Monte de Plata which stands behind today's Puerto Plata. Finally they reached El Golfo de las Flechas, so called because, once again, the Indians tried to resist, and failed. It is today's Gulf of Samaná, the eastern end of Hispaniola. And on January 18, 1493, the two caravels, heavily laden, took their leave of "Asia."

We have seen that in these Caribbean latitudes the trades blow constantly out of the east, and since a squarerigger cannot sail close to the wind, Columbus spent the rest of January tacking to the northeast in order to catch the wind for home: One more proof that he understood the Atlantic gyre. On January 21 he noted that the nights grew longer "because of the narrowing of the sphere," so he was not such a bad cosmographer after all, and on February 3 he noted that the North Star stood high. On February 4 his knowledge of the winds paid off: He caught the wind out of the west. He probably planned to run down the latitude of the constellation Auriga, which then shone in the evening, headed by Capella, one of the brightest navigational stars. Like all good zephyrs the west wind came with a storm, and on the night of February 13 *Niña* lost sight of *Pinta* in the gale. Striking all sails, Columbus dropped a sealed coffer into the sea containing a short relation of his voyage, lest his discovery be lost with him. The coffer has yet to be found. On February 15 he made it into the port of Santa María in the Azores.

The Portuguese used to return from Africa by sailing out this far in order to catch the west wind, so it took Columbus a while to convince the Portuguese governor that *Niña* had not been poaching on Portugal's African preserves. Impatiently, he began to write his first American letter, and on February 24, he set sail again and had to ride out another gale. Finally, on March 3, running before a strong wind under spritsail alone, he saw the full moon shine on Portugal's coast, which he wisely followed south at a safe distance. The next day, he anchored in the broad mouth of the Tagus, which forms the port of Lisbon, and immediately dispatched his letter by courier to the Spanish Court.

In regal Lisbon, Columbus insisted on being treated as an Admiral. On March 5 Bartolomeo Dias, who had been the first to round the Cape of Good Hope, came aboard the caravel and asked Columbus to come to his nao and explain his presence. Columbus replied that an Admiral of Castile neither presented himself on another's ship, nor sent anyone else; but he did condescend to show Dias his credentials. Dias backed down and welcomed the Admiral with a brass band. Columbus requested an audience with King João, not only to ask his help, but surely also to remind him that he had rejected a good project; a risky demonstration, for Dom João had just had his brother-in-law murdered for reasons of state, and he certainly would not have been pleased to see that his Castilian cousins had succeeded where he had failed even to try. But the King was wise enough to receive Columbus kindly, and he ordered *Niña* to be repaired without charge. Nevertheless, Columbus could not drop his guard, and during their conversation on the 9th of March, the King suggested that perhaps, according to his agreement with the Catholic Sovereigns, the newly found lands might belong to him. Columbus avoided the question and simply answered that, following orders, he had been careful not to call at

An Indian woman is used as a measure to show the extraordinary size of American palm leaves.

Pietro Martire Anghiera, Historia de L'Inde Occidentale, Vinegia, 1534

33

A hammock. These were unknown in Europe but soon were adopted by sailors as a novel and comfortable way of sleeping on board.
Pietro Martire Anghiera, Historia de L'Inde Occidentale, Vinegia, 1534

any of Portugal's African ports, and the King concluded that "no third party" need intervene in this discussion. Rui de Pina, Dom João's chronicler, tells an interesting story: the King asked one of Columbus' Indian guides to map his home islands on the table with some beans, and then asked another to do the same. He was delighted to find that the two "maps" were identical.

On March 13 the Admiral left Lisbon for Palos. He crossed the bar of the Saltés River on the 15th, and made port where he had first weighed anchors. In all, he had spent about a month sailing from the Canaries to San Salvador, three in the Antilles, one to the Azores, and one more to Lisbon and Palos. Six months for a leap as long as those of Jason and Odysseus to the extremes of the Mediterranean and the Black Sea, and also as long as Armstrong's to the moon. Independently, *Pinta* made Palos the same day, after sailing from Hispaniola directly to Bayona in Galicia, where, as Columbus feared he might do, Martín Alonso Pinzón had requested an audience with the King and Queen, but they had refused to receive him without the Admiral. Pinzón was ill (some say he brought syphilis from America), and in less than a month he was dead. The expedition could not have been put together without him, and he was actually the first to confirm the sighting of the "Indies" and to bring news of it to Europe; but he was not loyal to the Admiral, and Providence did not forgive him.

Columbus spent two weeks fulfilling his religious duties at La Rábida and at Holy Week in Seville. There, on Easter Sunday, he received their Catholic Majesties' reply to his letter from Lisbon. Addressed to the "Admiral and Viceroy," their letter already spoke of the next voyage, and Columbus, in his answer, began to expound on his ideas as colonizer. Then, picking up his two sons in Córdoba, where the good Beatriz had been a mother to both, he proceeded to Barcelona accompanied by a triumphal procession which included Indians carrying gold ornaments, monkeys, and parrots. They must all have felt the cold. On April 20, 1493, the Discoverer appeared before his satisfied Sovereigns in the great arched hall of El Tinell, still today an impressive setting in Barcelona's Gothic quarter. There, he was granted the privilege of quartering his crest with the arms of the kingdoms of Castile and Aragon on a field of islands and anchors.

It was Columbus' hour of triumph, a triumph which would stand in history, but which would not be his for long; for even as he settled down to plan his second voyage, his letter fired the imagination of discoverers everywhere. It was not long before the "dark and infinite Ocean" became a highway for fleet after fleet fitted out not only by adventurers, but also by investors whose agreements included insurance and dividends. In a sense, the letter launched modern capitalism, and not only that: In the long run it forced Europe, which had been accustomed to relying on prophetic or legendary texts, as in Columbus' *Book of Prophecies,* to accept a continental surprise which no one could have foreseen. From then on, America's motto would be "Show me," and the rest of the western world would soon adopt as well.

VI. THE CARIBBEAN AND THE WORLD

In three more voyages Columbus discovered practically all of the Caribbean except the Spanish Main, which Ojeda, Vicente Yañez Pinzón, and Bastidas explored in the meantime.

His second voyage, the colonizing enterprise he had foreseen in the Barcelona Letter, set sail from Cádiz via Gomera in 1493. Seventeen ships or more made up a proud fleet with pennants snapping in the breeze. Faithful *Niña* was along, and *Mariagalante,* a flagship of some two hundred *toneles* headed the fleet, which carried seeds, tools, cattle, twenty horses, and some twelve hundred colonists including friars, but no women. Juan de la Cosa was on board, as were the father and the uncle of Bartolomé de las Casas, the future defender of the Indians, and Alonso de Ojeda, who would be the second discoverer. Also Diego Columbus, the Admiral's youngest brother. In three weeks, and on a Sunday (hence the name) the fleet sighted the island of Dominica, its cliffs crowned by a jungle like a lion's mane. Then it threaded the bright necklace of the Lesser Antilles up to the island of San Juan, which later switched names with its capital city, Puerto Rico. Thence it pressed on to Hispaniola and Navidad, where it was supposed that forty Spaniards waited, their coffers full of gold. But when Columbus dropped anchor and fired his cannon, there was no reply. And when he went ashore he found that the fort had been burned down, and there were no survivors. The fleet surgeon, Chanca, examined Guacanagarí, who lay in a hammock claiming to have been wounded while defending his Spanish allies, but not a scratch was visible beneath his bandages; nevertheless Columbus remained faithful to his policy of making allies out of the Indians, and forgave him.

Columbus turned back along the northern coast of Hispaniola, and after twenty-five days beating against the wind, the colonists were exhausted, and Columbus was forced to make an unfortunate choice for the site of Isabella, his new colony: the first shelter he found. There, Ojeda and Margarit began to harass the Indians of the Cibao, and Columbus, after dispatching twelve ships to Spain, left his brother Diego in charge, and sailed west to explore the southern coast of Cuba. Then he turned back to explore lofty Jamaica. Meanwhile, emissaries began to come and go between Spain and America, and they reported at court that Diego was abusing his authority. On his return, Columbus tried to

appease the unruly colonists by abandoning his benevolent policy toward the Indians, and authorizing the first *encomiendas,* a pseudo-legal form of servitude; to no avail, for the Spaniards continued to rebel. Finally, in 1496, after experiencing his first hurricane, the Admiral set sail for home via Guadeloupe in *Niña,* with *India,* the first caravel built in America, in company. Elder brother Bartholomew, more capable than Diego, was left to found the new capital, Santo Domingo.

For his third voyage (1498–1500) the Admiral weighed anchors in Seville, and proceeded via Madeira and the Cape Verde Islands with two hundred men and three ships, plus another three that sailed directly to Santo Domingo. In three weeks Columbus made his landfall in Trinidad, and for the first time explored part of the mainland, the peninsula of Paria in today's Venezuela. That this "earthly paradise," as he called it, was part of a continent was clear to him from the volume of fresh water that flows from the mouths of the Orinoco, but, anxious to arrive in Santo Domingo, he simply called it "Another World," and embarked on one of his greatest feats of dead reckoning: he sailed direct from the island of Margarita to Santo Domingo, crossing a whole new sea, the Caribbean, from an unknown point to a fixed destination. In Santo Domingo matters had gone from bad to worse. Francisco Roldán, *alcalde mayor* of Hispaniola, had mounted an open rebellion against the Admiral, and Columbus was forced to hang several Spaniards. Too late: What little authority the Admiral still had disappeared with the arrival of the inquisitor Francisco de Bobadilla, who sent Columbus and his brothers back to Cádiz under arrest on the caravel *Gorda.* In the meantime, the Admiral had been candid enough to send to Spain from Santo Domingo a map (now lost), and more than a hundred pearls from the island of Margarita, and thanks to that map he began to lose first his monopoly, starting with Ojeda, and with it his authority. Nevertheless, he managed to put together one final voyage.

The Admiral, by then no longer Viceroy, called his fourth and last voyage (1502–1504) the "high voyage." He set sail from Cádiz and Gran Canaria with four ships and one hundred and forty men, among them Ferdinand Columbus, aged twelve, who told the story in his "Life of the Admiral"; and in three weeks they sighted Martinique and sailed to Santo Domingo. There, Columbus recognized the signs of the first hurricane of the season, but his warning was ignored by the new governor, Obando, who refused to allow the Admiral ashore and lost his great treasure fleet in the Mona Strait, where it is time someone found its remains. The Admiral weathered the storm, then continued westward along the southern coast of Cuba and crossed to the island of Bonacca in the gulf of Honduras. There, Indians in a luxurious canoe invited him farther west, but he preferred not to sail on downwind; rightly so, because it took him twenty-eight days to beat back along the coast to Cape Gracias a Dios where, "Thank God!," he finally put the wind on his beam. However, his sailor's prudence cost him the chance of discovering Yucatán and probably Mexico; the wings of destiny sometimes brush even great men too lightly.

In his fifties now, and ill, Columbus imagined he heard across the Isthmus the roar of another Sea "which would lead to the Ganges." He insisted on searching for a passage across Central America, which, if this were Asia, might be Marco Polo's Malacca Strait. But destiny once more eluded him; if he had sailed up the San Juan river in Nicaragua, or the Chagres in Panama, he could have walked to where he would have seen the Pacific. In the river of Belén, some sixty miles west of Panama, the Indians, under the Quibián, finally mounted a full-scale offensive and succeeded in expelling the Spaniards by force. One of Columbus' ships remained aground on the bar of the river, and another had to be abandoned later in Portobello. His two remaining ships were worm-eaten "like honeycombs," but the Admiral rightly insisted on sailing farther east, while his crews, worn out, insisted that it was time to turn north for Santo Domingo. The last night on the continent was spent below a cape which, because of its striated appearance, Columbus named Cabo Marmóreo (Marble Head), and which, according to Ferdinand, seemed to be the "end of the continent." This, I am sure, is the tight little anchorage that we Colombians call Zapzurro, below Cape Tiburón, the only high and striated cape on this whole coast. Heading north at last, the Admiral stopped for water at the Cayman Islands, sailed on to Cuba, and, unable to make Santo Domingo, beached his two last ships on the sands of today's Saint Ann's Bay, Jamaica. There he spent a year, impressing the Indians by foretelling the moon's eclipse of February 29, 1504. Finally, Méndez and Fieschi made a heroic voyage to Santo Domingo in a canoe. From there the Admiral returned to Spain for the last time in a chartered ship, with the last hundred survivors of *"el alto viaje"*.

In the end, where did Columbus really think he had been? In 1493, during his second voyage, he made his crews certify that Cuba was the eastern cape of Asia, so the Lesser Antilles must be the scores of islands which always rode ahead of Cathay (Cuba) and Cipango (Hispaniola) in contemporary maps, such as Behaim's globe. During his third voyage Columbus did write to the Sovereigns of "Another World," but it seems clear that he meant Behaim's Cattigara, the southern part of Asia, which our comparative map shows that La Cosa moved to the west; had the Admiral realized that he had found a totally new continent, would he not have given it and its "Indians" a new name, which he so loved to do? In 1502, he wrote Pope Alexander VI that he had discovered three hundred and thirty-three leagues of the Asian continent, which fits pretty closely the thousand miles of continental America which he had explored: both coasts of the Paria Peninsula in Venezuela during his third voyage, and Central America from Honduras to Colombia during his fourth. In his account of his fourth voyage he said that nine days west of Central America, which he called Veragua, lay Ciguare, a province of Cathay where people dressed luxuriously and had plenty of gold, horses, and ships with guns. This Ciguare, he said, was bathed by a sea, nine days beyond which flowed the river Ganges; a fairly good description of China and the Indian Ocean. But how far was "nine days?" Since Columbus' transatlantic voyage took about a month, nine days could mean about a third of the transatlantic distance, and if we measure off this distance on Behaim's globe, we come to Behaim's Ciamba (Ciguare?), which contains the cities of Zaitún and Quinsay; and if we do it again we just about reach Behaim's Ganges. So, Columbus left the concept of a really "New World" to Vespucci, who used the phrase in his *Mundus Novus*" letter, which was published in Florence around 1506.

In Spain, though he wrote that "his malady," probably arthritis, was beginning to paralyze his hands, Columbus initiated a long correspondence with his son, Diego, in which he fell back on his love for his family: "take good care of your brother . . . never did I find truer friends than my brothers" he wrote, and signed off as "your father who loves you as much as he loves himself." Columbus was disillusioned, but not poor, for out of the treasure of the Indies, the King, who was to outlive him by ten years, consistently paid him ten percent of the twenty percent that he, the King, received. But Columbus insisted until the end on the literal reading of his *Capitulaciones,* which stipulated that he was to receive ten percent of *all* the treasure that came from the Indies; impossible.

Less than three weeks after Columbus' return from his last voyage, Queen Isabella died in Medina del Campo. The King, who had just entered into possession of Naples, soon remarried and was in no hurry to receive Columbus. The Queen, wrote the Admiral to Diego, would surely remember him in her will. The Queen did remember her new subjects: "I pray the King and command my heirs that they see to it that the Indians who live in the said islands and Terra Firma shall not be harmed either in their persons or in their property, and that they be treated well and with justice. And that whatever harm has been done to them be remedied." But she did not mention Columbus. So much for another romantic legend. Columbus, on the other hand, did remember Beatriz, who outlived him by fourteen years. In his will of May 19, 1506, he instructed his heir, Diego, to provide for her, "for reasons which weigh heavily upon my soul, but which it is not fitting to mention here."

On the 20th of May, 1506, Columbus died in a dark house in Valladolid. He was attended only by his two sons, his brother Diego, now a friar, and Méndez and Fieschi, his most faithful servants, one a Spaniard and the other Genoese. No bishop accompanied him to his grave, nor any delegate of the Crown.

Columbus was buried in Valladolid, but in 1509 (some say 1513) his remains were transferred to the Carthusian Monastery of Las Cuevas in Seville, where, in 1526, they were joined by those of his son and heir, Diego. Diego had several times insisted that the Admiral wished to be buried in Hispaniola, and in 1538 the remains of father and son were sent to Santo Domingo at the request of Doña María de Toledo, Diego's widow. Also buried there were Luis, Columbus' polygamous grandson who died in 1575, and Luis' brother, Cristóbal. For two and a half centuries Columbus rested (at last!) in Santo Domingo, but when in 1795 Spain ceded

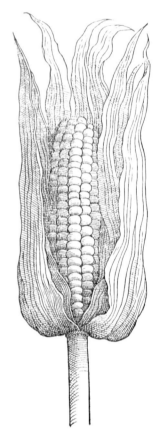

The first botanical description of maize was published after Columbus' second voyage in 1494. It was grown in Europe relatively early, probably from seed, and was easily accepted because of its visual similarity to old-world grains.

Pietro Martire Anghiera, Historia de L'Inde Occidentale, Vinegia, 1534

The great size of American trees was a new-world wonder centuries before the discovery of the California redwoods.

Pietro Martire Anghiera, Historia de L'Inde Occidentale, Vinegia, 1534

Santo Domingo to France under the treaty of Basel, Columbus sailed again to create his last riddle. The casket from Santo Domingo first went to Havana to escape the French, and then to Seville, in 1899, to escape Teddy Roosevelt's Americans. But in the meantime, in 1877, another casket, which clearly seemed to be the original, was found near the altar of the Cathedral of Santo Domingo, and the arguments began. I, for one, believe the Admiral of the Ocean Sea lies in the Cathedral of his beloved Hispaniola, the island he loved, the island which was denied him. But the Discoverer still has two monumental graves, one in Seville and the other in Santo Domingo.

In 1507, only a year after Columbus' death, Martin Waldseemüller of the Monastery of St. Dié, fascinated by the best-selling letters of Amerigo Vespucci which quickly reached almost three times as many editions as the Barcelona Letter, gave the New World its name. It should have been Colombia, but history can be as ungrateful to discoverers as modern universities to inventors. Nevertheless, Vespucci was not to blame for the name, and Columbus always spoke well of him. Most important, Waldseemüller in his map not only drew a new Ocean on the other side of America, but into it he moved "Cipangu," Japan. So, thanks to Vespucci's letters and to the cartographer of St. Dié, Europe saw a map of the Pacific six years before Balboa actually reached its shores, although it remained unbaptized until Magellan finally crossed it. History moves in spurts, and whereas Columbus' austere Barcelona Letter was the first press release of the Discovery, it was Vespucci's letters, often salted with sex and improbably paired with the cartography of a monk from St. Dié, which gave the discovery real publicity in the yellow press of the time.

Nevertheless, the Barcelona Letter so transformed contemporary geography that, in order to prevent conflict between the two discoverer nations, on May 3 and 4, 1493, Pope Alexander VI was obliged to promulgate Papal Bulls that divided the globe between Spain and Portugal along the longitude that passes "a hundred leagues to the west of the Azores and the Cape Verdes" (approximately 30 degrees West), a line which was later moved farther west by the Treaty of Tordesillas, unwittingly giving Brazil to Portugal. In the Spanish hemisphere, Columbus "invented" another world; in Latin, the same word means to discover and to invent. But instead of heathen Emperors and wealthy Mandarins, he found Paradise. The beautiful, naked Indians came out of the sea and took him by the hand; and he dressed them, honored them, and fell in love with them. But the idyll could not last, for two such disparate ways of life could not be fused with impunity, and the tragedy started with the ambivalence of both. In the letter, Columbus pointed out that the Indians could easily be made to work; the Indians, on the other hand, begged to be taken along by the "men from heaven," but once on board, thought only of escape. Perhaps if the nao *Santa María* had not been wrecked in Haiti, forty Spaniards would not have been left behind for almost a year to range the countryside, grabbing women and gold at will, and the Indians would not have destroyed their fort, La Navidad. If there had been no confrontation, Columbus might have returned to Hispaniola with his thousand colonists to the welcome he thought he deserved; Ojeda and Margarit might never have mounted their punitive expeditions against the Indians of the Cibao; and Columbus might never have had to make the distinction between "good" Indians and "bad," who could be enslaved. If, if, if.

It is an ill wind which blows no good, and had the Spaniards not intervened, the aggressive Caribs would probably have completely conquered the Taínos, and perhaps even the mainland Indians, who were so in tune with nature that the animals they portrayed in gold were all beautiful, while gods and men almost always looked ferocious. But in the end, for both Caribs and Taínos, the ill wind prevailed.

Queen Isabella begged and commanded that her Indian subjects be respected. Bartolomé de las Casas, a barefoot friar, scolded the Imperial Council of the Indies for its neglect of the Emperor's new subjects: "Verily I fear for your souls," he wrote, sending a victorious empire into a crisis of conscience which has no parallel in history. But in 1537 the Pope still felt it necessary to decree that Indians had souls. Columbus and Guacanagarí, his first Indian ally, conserved their friendship for years, and one of the Indian interpreters from the first voyage, baptized "Don Diego," stayed with Columbus through the second. Nevertheless, the Indians' world would soon be gone forever, except for a few "little" things like a hammock by the sea, a whiff of tobacco, and a bite of cassava bread.

But we have seen that Columbus made his second landfall in the Caribbean almost exactly where the Indians of the first voyage had indicated, and one wonders who was the best geographer, Columbus or his Indian guides. This was to be the voyage which would fulfill the Barcelona Letter's promise of peace and prosperity. Paradise was not yet lost: Twenty ships ride at anchor in a quiet bay, their mast-tops drawing lazy circles among the small clouds. The hilltops suddenly light up as the sun dies, then the sea gives up its azure to the sky, which, as the stars reclaim their infinity, quickly turns black. A thousand rough Spanish voices intone the Salve Regina. The graceful Indians haul their canoes up onto the beach, their hair flying in the breeze like a pony's mane. They wave and cry the first Spanish word they have learned: "*Almirante!*"

FURTHER READING

Bernáldez, Andrés, *Memorias del reinado de los Reyes Católicos.* Contained in *Raccolta di Documemti e Studi*, Cesare de Lollis, ed., Genoa, 1892.

Boletín de la Academia de Historia, Bogotá, July 1988, "Colón, La China y El Japón. La Primera Recalada del Descubridor," by Mauricio Obregón.

Charlier, George A., *Étude complète de la navégation de Cristóbal Colón*, livre 1er. Bibliothèque de Belgique, 1988.

Colón, Fernando, *Vida del Almirante*. Mexico, 1947.

Encounter '92, March 1989. (Neal Sealey.) Nassau, Bahamas.

Fernández de Oviedo, Gonzalo, *Historia General y Natural de las Indias*. 1535.

First San Salvador Conference. (Taviani, Durlacher, Wolper, Kelley, Gerace, Hoffman, Winter.) Bahamian Field Station, 1986.

Gil Juan, and Varela, Consuelo (eds.), *Cartas de particulares a Colón y relaciones coetáneas*. Madrid, 1984.

———(ed.), *El libro de Marco Polo con apostillas de Colón*. Madrid, 1988.

Gracia Franco, Salvador, *La legua náutica en la edad media*. Madrid, 1957.

Herrera, Antonio de, *Historia General de los hechos de los castellanos en las Islas y Tierra Firme del Mar Océano*, 1535.

Journal of Sedimentary Petrology, September, 1985. "Diagenesis of Quarternary Bahamian Beachrock," by J.A. Beier.

Las Casas, Barcolomé de, *Historia de Las Indias*. 1550–1563.

Martínez-Hidalgo, José María, *Columbus' Ships*. Barre, Massachusettes, 1966.

Mitchell, Steven, and Keegan, William, *Archaeological Evidence for Determining Christopher Columbus' Voyage through the Bahamas, 1492.* Earthwatch, 1987.

Morison, Samuel Eliot, *Admiral of the Ocean Sea.* Boston, 1942.

————, and Obregón, Mauricio, *The Caribhbean as Columbus Saw It.* Boston, 1964.

National Geographic Magazine, November, 1986. (Joseph Judge.)

Nûnez Jiménez, Antonio, *El almirante de la tierra más hermosa.* Cádiz, 1985.

Obregón, Mauricio, *Argonauts to Astronauts.* New York, 1980.

————, *Colón en el mar de los caribes. Historia, geografía, y náutica del descubrimiento.* Bogotá, 1990.

Oceanus, Fall 1987. "New Calculations Point Again to San Salvador," by Philip L. Richardson and Roger A. Goldsmith.

Peck, Douglas T., *Reconstruction of the Columbus Log from a Sailor-Navigator Viewpoint.* Society for the History of Discoveries, 1988.

Terrae Incognitae, Vol. XV. Wayne State University Press, 1983.

Varela, Consuelo (ed.), *Cristóbal Colón: textos y documentos completos.* Madrid, 1984.

THE CATALAN ATLAS OF 1375

MAP OF THE WORLD BY ABRAHAM CRESQUES,
MASTER OF THE MAJORCAN SCHOOL, C. 1375.
KNOWN AS THE CATALAN ATLAS (INK AND COLOR ON SIX
VELLUM DIPTYCHS,
64 × 300 CM., BIBLIOTHÈQUE NATIONALE, PARIS).

Commissioned by Peter of Aragon as a gift for Charles V of France, the Catalan Atlas is the showpiece of medieval cartography. In the two introductory diptychs at right, it summarizes the current knowledge of cosmology. The map itself, overleaf, uses information on China newly derived from Marco Polo and depicts the Indian subcontinent more accurately than Ptolemaic renderings, and pays uncommon attention to inland cities and foreign peoples. The Atlas is here reproduced from the flawless facsimile in the Institut Cartogràfic de Catalunya.

43

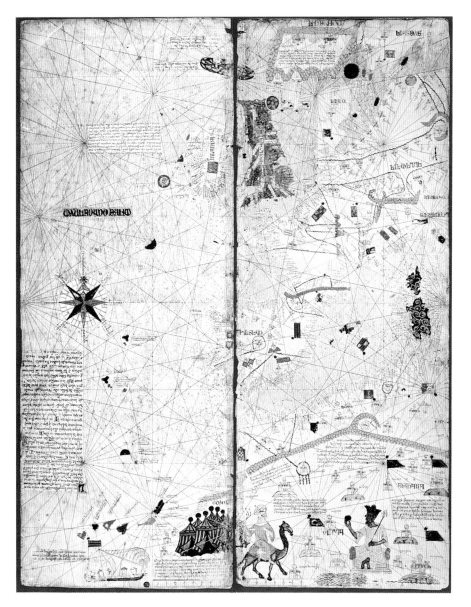

44

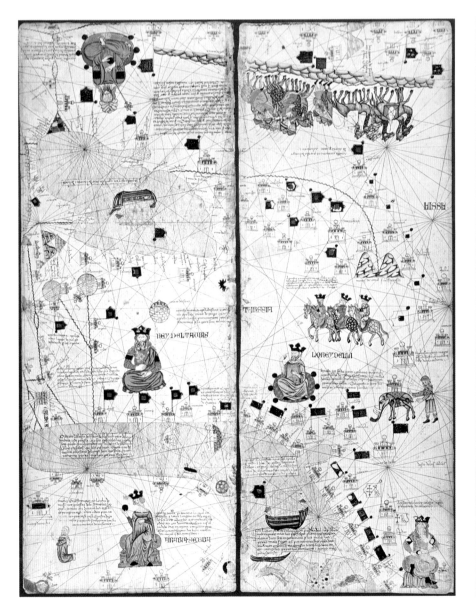

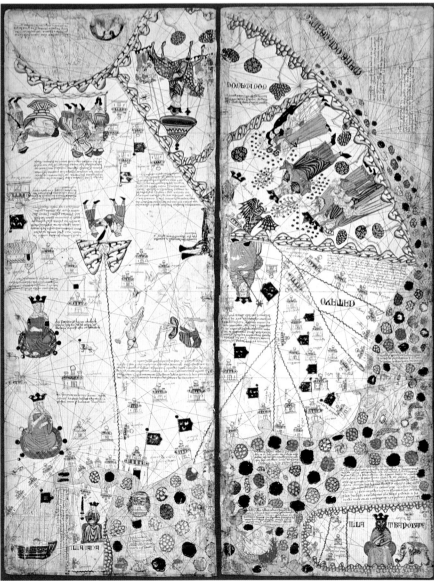

45

PTOLEMAIC MAPPAMUNDI

*This is one of the more colorful examples of the standard
late-medieval view of the world, which was based on
complex projections devised by the Alexandrian philosopher
Claudius Ptolemy in the second century. Although such maps
were surprisingly accurate for the time (the thick yellow lines
represent mountain ranges), the Ptolemaic system
underestimated the circumference of the globe by about one
quarter. Columbus used his own miscalculations as a primary
argument for the possibility of reaching Asia by sailing west.
Thus the actual distance to America nearly coincided with
his expectations, and he never realized that he had discovered
a new continent—though he did ultimately sense that it was
"another world,"* otro mundo, *possibly the Garden of Eden,
which was thought to lie at the eastern extreme
of Asia.*

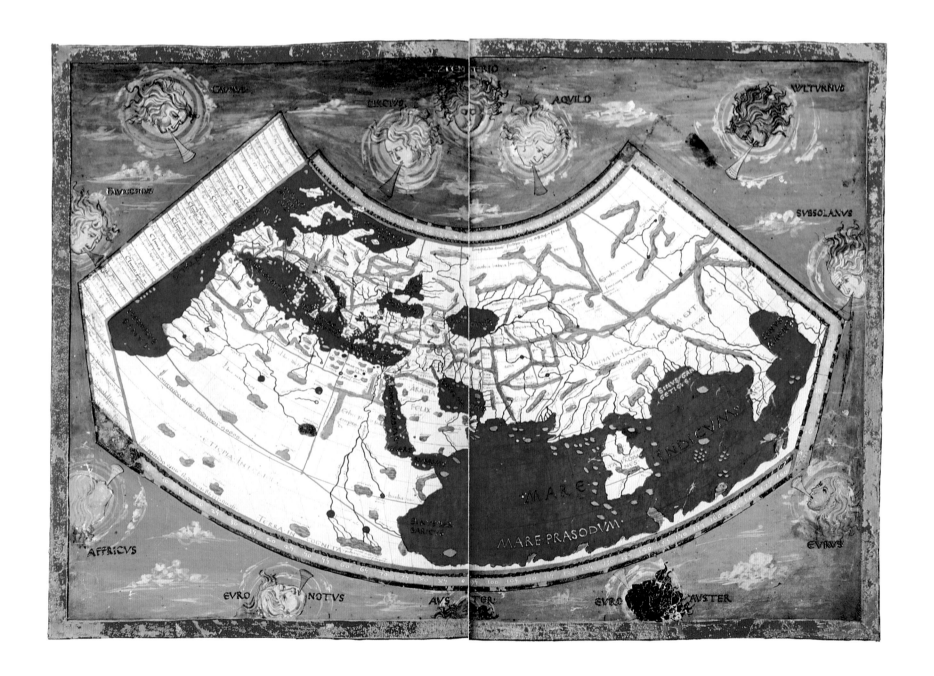

49

The Barcelona Letter of 1493

FACSIMILE OF THE COPY IN
THE NEW YORK PUBLIC LIBRARY

Epistola de insulis nuper inventis . . .
[Spanish] [Barcelona, Pedro Posa, after 4
March 1493] Folio, four pages, 29.05 × 21.3 cm. sole
extant copy. Rare Books and Manuscripts Division.

SEÑOR por que se que aureis plazer dela grand vitoria que nuestro señor me ha dado en mi viaje vos escriuo esta por la ql sabreys como enxxxviii dias pase A las idias cō la armada q̄ los illustrissimos Rey e Reyna ñros señores me dieron dōdeyo falle muy muchas Islaspobladas cō gente sin numero: y dellas todas he tomado posesion por sus altezas con pregon y vādera rreal estendida y non me fue cōtradicho Ala primera q̄ yofalle puse nōbre sant saluador a comemoracien d̄su alta mages tat el qual marauillosamēte todo esto andado los idios la llaman guanaham Ala segūda puse nōbre la isla d̄ santa maria deconcepcion ala tercera ferrandina ala quarta la isla bella ala quita la Isla Juana e asi a cada vna nōbre nueuo Quando yo llegue ala Juana seg ui io la costa della al poniente yla falle tan grāde q̄ pense que seria tierra firme la prouicia de catayo y como no falle asi villas y luguares ēla costa dela mar saluo pequeñas poblaciones con lagente d̄las q̄les nopodia hauer fabla por q̄: luego fuyan todos:andaua yo a de lante por el dicho camino pēsādo deuo errar grādes Ciudades o villas y al cabo de muchas leguas visto q̄ no hauia inouació i que la costa me leuaua alsetētrion de adōde mi voluntad era cōtraria porq̄ el yuierno era ya ēcarnado yo tenia proposito d̄hazer del al austro y tan biē el viēto medio adelāte determine deno aguardar otro tiēpo y bolui atras fasta vn señalado puer to d̄ adōde ēbie dos hōbres por la tierra para saber si hauia Rey o grādes Ciudades ādoui erō tres iornadas yhallarō iñitas poblaciōes pequeñas i gēte si numero mas no cosa d̄reg imiēto por lo qual sebol uierō yo entēdia harto d̄ otros idios q̄ ia tenia tomados como conti nuamēte esta tierra era Isla e asi segui la costa della al oriēte ciento i siete leguas fasta dōde fa zia fin d̄l qual cabo vi otra Isla al oriēte disticta d̄ esta diez o ocho leguas ala qual luego puse nōbre la española y fui alli y segui la parte d̄l setentrion asi como d̄la iuana al oriēte. clxxviii grādes leguas por lina recta del oriēte asi como d̄la iuana la qual y todas las otras sō fortissimas en demasiado grado y esta enestremo en ella ay muchos puertos ēla costa d̄la mar sin cōparació de otros q̄ yo sepa en cristianos y fartos rrios y buenos y grandes q̄ es mara villa las tierras della sō altas y ē ella muy muchas sierras y mōtañas altissimas sin cōparació de la isla d̄ cētre frē to das f rmosissimas de mil fechuras y todas ādabiles y llenas de arbols d̄ mil maneras i altas i parecen q̄ llegā al cielo i tēgo pordicho q̄ iamas pierdē lafoia segun lo puede cōpbēder q̄ los vi tā verdes i tā hermosos como sō por mayo en spaña i dellos staua flor ridos dellos cō fruto i dellos enotratermino segū es su calidad i cātaua el rui señor i otros pa xaricos d̄mil maneras en el mes d̄nouiēbre por alli dōde io ādaua ay palmas de seis o de ocho maneras q̄ es admiracion vellas por la diformidad fermosa d̄ellas mas asicomo los o otros arboles y frutos eteruas en ella ay pinares amarauilla eay cāpiñas grādissimas eay mi el i de muchas maneras de aues y frutas muy diuersas ēlas tierras ay muchas minas deme tales eay gēte istimable numero La spañola es marauilla la sierras ylas mōtañas y las uegas ylas campiñas y las tierras tan fermosas ygruesas para plātar ysēbrar pacriar ganados de to das suertes para hedificios de villas elugares los puertos dela mar aqui no hauria creēcia sin vista ydelos rios muchos y grandes y buenas aguas los mas delos quales traē oro ē los arbo les y frutos e yeruas ay grandes differencias d̄ aquel las d̄la iuana en esta ay muchas speçie rias y grandes minas de oro y de otros metales. La gente desta isla y todas las otras q̄ he hallado y hauido: ni aya hauido noticia andan todos desnudos hōbres y mugeres asi como sus madres los parē hauū que algunas mugeres se cobrian vn solo lugar cō vna foia de yerua:o vna cosa dealgodō q̄pa ello fazen ellos no tienen fierro ni azero ni armas nison par t accllo no por que no sea gente bien dispuesta y de fermosa estatura saluo que sō muy temoroso amarauilla no tienē otrasarmas saluo las armas d̄las cañas quando estan cōla simiente qual ponen al cabo vn palillo agudo eno osan vsar d̄aqllas que m ... vezes m ... ē ... embiar auera dos o tres hombres alguna villa pa hauer fabl y saliē ...

si numero: y despues q̃ les verã llegar fuyan a no aguardar padre a hijo y esto no por que a nj
guno se aya hecho mal antes a todo cabo adõde yo aya estado y podido hauer fabla les he da
do de todo loque tenia asi paño como otras cosas muchas sĩ recebir por ello cosa algũa mas
sõ asi temerosos sin remedio: verdad es que despues que aseguran y pierdẽ este miedo ellos son
tanto sĩ engaño y tan liberales delo q̃ tienẽ que no locreerian sino el q̃lo viese: ellos de cosa que
tẽgan pidiẽdogela iamas dizẽ deno antes cõuidan lapsona cõ ello y muestran tãto amor que
darian los corazones y quierẽ sea cosa deualor quien sea depoco precio luego por qual quj̃e
ra cosica de qual quiera manera que sea q̃ sele depor ello sea cõtentos: yo defendi q̃ noseles d e
sen cosas tan siujles como pedazos de escudillas rotas y pedazos de vidrio roto y cabos dagu
getas: haũ que quãdo ellos esto podiã llegar les parescia hauer la meior ioya del mũdo. que
se acerto hauer vn marinero por vna agugeta de oro depeso de dos castellanos y medio: y otros
de otras cosas q̃ muy mates valiã mucho mas ya por blãcas nueuas dauan por ellas todo
quanto t nian haũ que fuese dos ni tres castellanos de oro o vna arrona o dos de algodõ fila
dõ fasta los pedazos delos arcos rotos delas pipas tomauan ydauan loq̃ tenian como besti
as asi que me parecio mal: yo lo defedi ydaua yo graciosas mil cosas buenas q̃ yo leuaua por
que tomen amor y alliẽde desto se farã cristianos que seidiuan al amor e ceruicio de sus altezas
y de toda la naciõ castellana: e procurã de aiũtar de nos dar delas cosas que tienẽ en abundã
cia que nos sõ necessarias y no conocian njguna seta nj idolatria saluo que todos creen q̃ las
fuerças yelbiẽ es encielo y creian muy firme que yo cõ estos nauios ygente venia del cielo yental
catamiento me recebian entodo cabo despues dehauer perdido elmiedo y esto no procede por q̃
sean ignorantes saluo demuy sotil igenio y õbres que nauegan todas aquellas mares que es
marauilla labuena cuenta q̃ ellos dan de todo saluo porque nũca vierõ gẽte vestida ni semeian
tes nauios yluego que legue alas indias dela pri mera isla q̃ halle tome pforza algunos dellos pa
ra que deprēdiesen yme diese noticia delo que auia en aquellas partes casi fue que luego ẽtendiõ
y nos aellos quando por lengua o señas: y estos han aprouechado mucho oy en dia los traigo
q̃ siẽpre estã deproposito q̃ vego del cielo por mucha cõuersaciõ q̃ ayan hauido cõmigo y estos
eran los primeros apronunciarlo adõde yo llegaua y los otros andauan corriendo decasa ẽ
casa: y alas villas cercanas cõ bozes altas venit: venit auer lagente del cielo asi todos õbres
como mugers despues dehauer elcoraçõ seguro de nos venia q̃ nõ cadaua grande ni pequeño
y todos trayaan algu decomer ydebeuer quedauan cõ vn amor marauilloso ellos tienẽ todas
las yslas muy muchas canoas amanera defustes dereno dellas maiores dellas menores y al
gunas: y muchas sõ mayores que bña fusta dediez ococho bãcos no sõ tan anchas porque sõ
dehun solo madero mas buna fusta no terna cõ ellas al remo porque van que no es cosa decre
er y cõ estas nauegan todas aquellas islas q̃ sõ inumerables: y tratẽ sus mecaderias: algunas
destas canoas he visto cõ lxx y lxxx õbres en ella y cada vno cõ su remo entodas estas islas no
vide mucha diuersidad dela fechura dela gente nĩ ẽ las costumbres nĩ enla lengua: saluo que
todos se entienden q̃ es cosa muy singular para lo que espero q̃ determinaran sus altezas para la
cõuersaciõ dellos de nuestra santa fe ala qual sõ muy dispuestos: ya dixe como yo hauia ãdado
c. vii leguas por la costa dela mar por laderecha liña de osidẽte a oriente por la isla iuana segũ el
qual camino puedo dezir que esta isla es maior que inglaterra yescosia iũntas por que allẽde des
tas c vii. leguas me queda dela parte deponiente dos prouincias que yo no he ãdado: launa de
las q̃les llaman auan: a dõde nasce la gente cõ cola las q̃les prouincias no pueden tener enlõgura
menos de. l. o lx. leguas segun puede entender destos indios qu yo traigo los q̃les saben todo s
las yslas esta otra española en cierco tiene mas que la españa toda desde colunya por costa de
mar fasta fuẽte rauia en viscaya pues en vna quadra andoue. dxxviii grandes leguas por rec
ta liñ a e occident a oriente esta es para desear: e v es para nunca dexar enla qual puesto
_as tenca tomar possessiõ por sus altezas y todas sean mas abastadas delo q̃ yo sé
_os las traigo por sus altezas que dellas _

se y puedo dezir ytodas las tengo por de sus altezas qual dellas pueden disponer como y tau cõ
plidamête como delos Reynos de castilla en esta española en ellugar mas cõuenible ymeior
comarca para las minas del oro ypetodo trato asi dela tierra firme deaqui como de aquella
dealla del gran can adõde haura grãdo trato eganancia hetomado possessiõ de vna villa grã
de ala qual puse nõbre la villa denauidad: yeu ella hefecho fuerza y fortaleza que ya aestasho
ras estara del todo acabada ybedexado enella gente que abasta para semeiante fecho cõ armas
y artellarias euituallas por mas de vn año yfusta ymaestro dela mar entodas artes para fazer
otras ygrandeamistad cõ el Rey de aquella tierra en tanto grado quese preciaua deme llamar y
etener por hermano ebaũ que le mudase la volũtad a hofender esta gête el nlos suios nosabê
que sean armas yandan desnudos como yabe dicho sõ los mas temerosos que ay en el mũdo
asique solamente la gente que alla queda es para destroir toda aquella tierra y es ysla sipeligro
de sus personas sabiendoseregir entodas estas islas me parece que todos los õbres sean cõtê
tos cõ vna muger i asu maioral o Rey dan fasta: veynte: las mugeres me parece que trabaxã
mas que los õbres ni hepodido entender sitenien bienes propios que me parecio ver q a aquello
que vno tenia todos hazian parte en especial delas cosas comederas en estas islas fasta aqui
no hehallado õbres mõstrudos cõmo muchos pensauan mas antes estoda gête demuy lindo
acatamiento ni sõ negros como ê guinea saluo cõ sus cabellos corredios ynosecrian adõdeay
i peto demasiado delos rayos solares es verdad quel sol tiene alli grãd fuerça puesto que esdi
distinta dela liña equinocial veite eseis grades en estas islas adõdeay mõtañas grandes: ay tenia
a fuerça el frio este yuierno: mas ellos lo sufrem porla costumbre que cõla ayuda delas viandas
comen cõ especias muchas y muy calientes enoemasia: asique mõstruos nobe hallado ninoti
cia saluo de vnaysla que es aqui enla segunda ala entrada delas yndias q es poblada devna
iente que tienê en todas las yslas por muy fezozes los qualles comê carne vmana estos tienê
muchas canaus cõlas quales corrê todas las yslas de idia roban ytomã quanto pueden ellos
no sõ mas disfozmes que los otros saluo q tienê encostumbre traer los cabellos largoscom
omugeres y vsan arcos y flechas delas mismas armas decañas cõ vn palillo alcabo porefec
to de fierzo q no tienê sõ fezozes entre estos otros pueblos que sõ enemasiado grado couardes
mas yo no los tengo en nada mas que alos: otros estos sõ aquellos q trata cõlas mugeres
dematrenomonio q es laprimera ysla partiendo despaña para las idias q se falla enla qual no ay
hõbreninguno: ellas no vsã exercio femenil saluo arcos y frechas como los sobre dichos de cañas
yseamiau cõlamues de arambre ocque tiene mucho otra ysla meseguran mayor q la
española euque las psonas no tienê ningũ cabello. En esta ay oro si cuento y destas y delas o
e ras traigo comigo idios para testimonio: e cõclusiõ afablar desto solamête quesea fecho este
viageque fuesi de corria que puede vesus altezas q̃yo les dare oro quanto omiesê menester con
muy poquita ayuda q̃ sus altezas medara agora ipeciaria y algodõ quãto sus altezas mãdarã
cargar y almastica quãta mandaran cargar e:dela qual fasta oy no seha fallado saluo eu gre
cia enla ysla de xio y el señorio la uende como quiere y liguñaloe quãto mandaran cargar y es
clauos quãtos mãdaran cargar e serau:delos ydolatres y creo hauer fallado ruybaruo.y caue
la e otras mil cosas deustancia fallare que hauran fallado la gête que yo ella dexo porque yo
nomebe detenido nigũ cabo eu quãto duiento me aia dado lugar:denauegar solamente en la
villa de nauidad enquanto dexe asegurado E bien asêtado E ala verdad mucho mas ficiera
si los nauios me siruieran como razõ demandaua Esto es harto y eterno dios n̄ nestro señor
el qual da a todos aquellos q̃ andan sucamino victoria de cosas que parecen imposibles:yesta
señaladamête fuela vna por q̃ hauñ que destas tierras aian fallado ⭕ escripto todo va por cõ
lectura sin allegar deuista saluo cõprendiendo a tanto que los oyêtes los mas escuchauan e
iuzgauan mas por fabla que por poca c̄ dello asi que pues nuestro: Redentor dio esta. vic
toria A nuestros Jllustrisimos rey :creyna casu reynos Famosos de a alta cosa A dõde toda

La christiandad deue tomar alegriay fazer grandes fiestasy dar gradas solēnes ala sancta tri
nidad cō muchas oraciones solēnes por el tanto enxalçamiento que hauran en tornandose
tantos pueblos a nuestra sancta fe :y despues por los bienes tēporals q̃ no solamēte ala españa
mas atodos los christianos ternan aqui refrigerio y ganancia esto segun el fecho a si en breue
fecha enla calauera sobre las yslas de canaria a xv de febrero año Mil. cccclxxxxiii.

       Fara lo que mandareys   El Almirāte

       Anima que venia dentro en la Carta.

Despues desta escripto:y estādo en mar de. Castilla salio tanto viēto cō migo.sul y sueste que
me ha fecho descargar los nauios po cori aqui en este puerto de lisbona oy que fue la mayor
marauilla del mundo adōde acorde escriuir asus altezas. entodaslas yndias he siempre halla
do y los tēporals como en mayo adōde yo fuy en xxxiidias y volui en xxviii salio quedas tormen
tas me ade tenido xiiii dias corriendo por esta mar:dizen aqua todos los bōbres dela marqa
mas ouo tan mal yuierno no ni tantas perdidas de naues fecha ha quatorze dias de marzo:

      ESTA Carta en bio Colom Alescriuano deraciō
      De las Jslas Halladas en Las Yndias: Lōtenida
      A Otra De Sus Altezas

The Barcelona Letter of 1493

TRANSCRIPTION OF THE ORIGINAL TEXT

SENOR por que se que aureis plazer dela grand vitoria que nuestro señor me ha dado en mi viaie vos escriuo esta por la ꝗel sabreys como enueinte dias pase A las ĩdias cõ la armada ꝗ los illustrissimos Rey e Reyna ñros señores me dieron dõdeyo falle muy muchas Yslas pobladas cõ gente sin numero: y dellas todas he tomado posesion por sus altezas con pregon y uãdera rreal estendida y non mefu e cõ tradicho Ala primera ꝗ yofalle pues noubre sant saluador a comemoracion desu alta mages tat el qual marauillosamente todo esto andado los ĩdios la llaman guanaham. Ala segũda puse nonbre la isla de santa maria deconcepcion ala tercera ferrandina ala quarta la isla bella ala quĩta la Ysla Juana e asi a cada vua nonbre nueuo Quando yo llegue ala Juana seg ui io la costa della al poniente yla falle tan grande ꝗ pense que seria tierra firme la prouĩcia de cataio y como no falle asi villas y luguares enla costa dela mar saluo pequeñas poblaciones con lagente delas ꝗules nopodia hauer fabla por que luego fuyan todos: andaua yo a de lante por el dicho camino pẽsãdo deuo errar grãdes Ciudades o villas y al cabo de muchas leguas visto ꝗ no hauia ĩnouaciõ i que la costa me leuaua alsetẽtriõ de adõde mi voluntad era cõtraria porꝗ el yuierno era ya ẽcarnado yo tenia proposito de hazer del al austro y tan biẽ el viẽto medio adelãte determine deno aguardar otro tiẽpo y bolui atras fasta vn señalado puer to de adõde ẽbie dos hõbres por la tierra para saber si hauia Rey o grãdes Ciudades ãdoui erõ tres iornadas yhallarõ ĩfinitas poblaciões pequeñas i gẽte sĩ numero mas no cosa dereg imiẽto porlo qual sebolnierõ yo entẽdia harto de otros ĩdios ꝗ ia tenia tomados como conti nuamẽte esta tierra era Ysla e asi segui la costa della al oriẽte ciento i siete leguas fasta dõde fa zia fin:del qual cabo vi otra Ysla al oriẽte distĩcta de esta diez o

ocho leguas ala qual luego puse nombre la spañola y fui alli y segui la parte del setentrion asi como dela iuana al oriente. clxxviii grãdes leguas por linia recta del oriẽte asi como dela iuana la qual y todas las otras sõ fortissimas en demasiado grado y esta enestremo en ella ay muchos puertos enla costa dela mar sĩ cõparaciõ de otros ꝗ yo sepa en cristianos y fartos rrios y buenos y grandes ꝗ es mara villa las tierras della sõ altas y ẽ ella muy muchas sierras y mõtañas altissimas sĩ cõparaciõ de la isla de cẽtre frei todas fermosissmas de mil fechuras y todas ãdabiles y llenas de arbol's de mil maneras i altas i parecen ꝗ llegã al cielo i tẽgo pordicho ꝗ iamas pierdẽlafoia segun lo puede cõphẽder ꝗ los vi tã verdes i tã hermosos como sõ por mayo en spaña i dellos stauã floridos dellos cõ fruto i dellos enotrotermino segũ es su calidad i cãtaua el ruiseñor i otros pa xaricos demil maneras en el mesdenouieubre por alli dõde io ãdaua ay palmas de seis ode ocho maneras ꝗ es admiracion verlas por la diformidad fermosa dellas mas asicomo los o otros arboles y frutos eiervas en ella ay pinares amarauilla eay canpiñas grãdissimas eay mi el i de muchas maneras de aues y frutas muy diuersas enlas tierras ay muchas minas deme tales eay gẽte ĩstimabile numero Laspañola es marauilla la sierras ylas mõtañas y las uegas ilas campiñas y las tierras tan fermosas ygruesas para plantar ysẽbrar pacriar ganados de to das suertes para hedificios de villas elugares los puertos dela mar aqui no hauria ꞓhencia sin vista ydelos rios muchos y grandes y buenas aguas los mas delos quales traẽ oro ẽ los arbõ les y frutos e yeruas ay grandes differencias de aquel las dela iuana en esta ay muchas specie rias y grandes minas de oro y de otros metales. Lagente desta ysla y detodas las otras ꝗ he fallado y hauido:ni haya hauido noticia andan todos desnudos hõbres y mugeres asi como sus madres los parẽ haun que algunas mugeres se cobiian vn solo lugar cõ vna foia

de yerr ua: o vna cosa de algodõ quepa ello fazen
ellos no tienen fierro ni azero ni armas nison par aello
no por que no sea gente bien dispuesta y de fermosa
estatura saluo que sõ muy temeroso amarauilla no
tienẽ otrasarmas saluo las [arm] as delas cañas
quando estan cõla simiente [a la] qual ponen al cabo
vn pa lillo agudo eno osan vsar de aq̃llas que [muchas
de] vezes [me ha aca]escido embiar atierra dos otros
hombres alguna villa pa hauer fabla i salir [a ellos
dellos] sĩ numero:y despues q̃ los veyã llegar fuyan a
no aguardar padre a hiio y esto no por que nĩ guno se
aya hecho mal antes a todo cabo adõde yo aya estado
y podido hauer fabla les heda do de todo loque tenia
asi paño como otras cosas muchas sĩ recebir por ello
cosa algũa mas sõ asi temerosos sin remedio:verdad es
que despues que aseguran y pierdẽ este miedo ellos
son tanto sĩ engaño y tan liberales delo q̃ tienẽ que no
locreerian sino el q̃lo viese:ellos de cosa que tẽgan
pidiẽdogela iamas dizẽ deno antes cõuidan lapsona cõ
ello y muestran tãto amor que darian los corazones y
quierẽ sea cosa deualor quien sea de poco precio
luego por qual quie ra cosica de qual quiera manera
que sea q̃ sele deporello seã cõtentos:yo defendi q̃
noseles diesen cosas tan siuiles como pedazos de
escudillas rotas y pedazos de vidrio roto y cabos dagu
getas:haũ que quãdo ellos esto podiã llegar los
parescia hauer lameior ioya del mũdo. que se acerto
hauer vn marinero por vna aguageta de oro depesode
dos castellanos y medio:yotros de otras cosas q̃ muy
menos valiã mucho mas ya por blãcas nueuas dauan
por ellas todo quanto tenian haũ que fuesẽ dos ni tres
castellanos de oro o vna arroua o dos de algodõ fila
do fasta los pedazos delos arcos rotos delas pipas
tomauan ydauan loq̃ tenian como besti as asi que me
parecio mal:yo lo defẽdi ydaua yo graciosas mil cosas
buenas q̃ yo leuaua por que tomen amor y allẽda
desto de farã cristianos que seĩclinan al amoreceruicio

de sus altezas y de toda la naciõ castellana:e procurã
de aiũtar de nos dar delas cosas que tenẽ en abundã
cia que nos sõ necessarias y no conocian nĩguna seta
ni idolatria saluo que todos creen q̃ las fuercas yelbiẽ
es eñlcielo y creian muy firme que yo cõestosnauios y
gentevenia del cielo yental catamiento me recebian
entodo cabo despues dehauer pdido elmiedo y esto
no procede porq̃ sean ignorantes saluo demuy sotil
ĩgenio y õbres que nauegan todas aquellas mares que
es marauilla labuena cuenta quellos dan de todosaluo
porquenũca vierõ gẽtẽ vestida nisemeian tes nauios
yluego que lege alas ĩdias ẽla primera isla q̃ halle tome
pforza algunos dellos pa ra que deprẽdiesen yme
diese notia delo que auia enaquellas partes easi fue
que luego ẽtendirõ y nos aellos quando por lengua
oseñas:yestos han aprouechado mucho oy endia los
traigo q̃ siẽpre estã deproposito q̃ vẽgo del cielo por
mucha cõversasiõ q̃ ayan hauido cõmigo y estos eran
los primeros apronunciarlo adonde yo llegaua y los
otros andauan corriendo decasa ẽ casa:y alas villas
cercauas cõ bozes altas venit:venit auer lagente del
cielo asi todos hõbres como mugeres despues dehauer
elcorazõ seguro de nos veniã q̃ nõ cadauã grande
nipequeño ytodos trayaan algu decomer ydebeuer
quedauan cõ vn amor maranilloso ellos tienẽ todas las
yslas muy muchas canoas amanera defustes dereino
dellas maioras dellas menores yal gunas: ymuchas sõ
mayores que hña fusta dediez eocho bãcos:nosõ tan
auchas porque sõ dehun solo madero mas huna fusta
noterna cõ ellas alremo porque van queno es cosa
decre er y cõ estas nauegan todas aquellas islas q̃ sõ
inumerables:ytratẽ sus mercaderias:algunas destas
canoas he visto cõ lxx ylxxx õbres enella y cada vno
cõ suremo entodas estas islas no vide mucha
diuersidad dela fechura dela gente ni en las
costumbres ni enla lengua:saluo que todos se
entienden q̃ escosa muy sĩgular para lo que espero q̃

determinaran sus altezas para la cõuersaciõ dellos de
nuestra santa fe ala qual sõ muydispuestos:ya dixe
como yohauia ãdado c.vii leguas porla costa dela mar
por laderecha liña deosidẽte aorieute por la isla iuana
segũ el qual camino puedo desir que esta isla esmaior
que inglaterra yescosia iuntas por que allẽde des tas c
vii. leguas me queda dela parte deponiente dos
prouĩsias que io nohe andado:lavna de las ǫeles
llaman anau:adõde nasẽ lagẽte cõcola las ǫeles
prouĩsias nopueden tener enlõgura menos de.l o
lx.leguas segun puede enteuder destos ĩdios qu yo
tengo los ǫels saben todo s las yslas esta otra española
encierco tiene mas que la españa toda desde colunya
por costa de mar fasta fuẽterauia en uiscaya pues en
vna quadra anduue clxxxviii grands leguas por rec ta
linia [de] occident a oriente esta es para desear:e
[vista] es para nunca dexar enla qual puesto [que de
todas] tenga tom [ado] possessiõ por sus altezas
ytodas sean mas abastadas delo que [.......................]
se y puedo dezir ytodas las tengo por de sus altezas
qual dellas pueden disponer como y taucõ plidamente
como delos Reynos de castilla eũ ẽsta española en
ellugar mas cõuenible ymeior comarca para las minas
del oro ydetodo trato asi dela tierra firme deaqua
como de a quella dealla del gran can adõde haura
grand trato eganancia hetomado possessiõ de vna villa
gran de ala qual puse nõbre la villa denauidad:yeu
ella hefecho fuerza y fortaleza que ya aestasho ras
estara del todo acabada yhedexado enella gente que
abasta para semeiante fecho cõ armas y artellarias e
vituallas por mas de vn año yfusta ymaestro dela mar
entodas artes para fazer otras ygrandeamistad cõ el
Rey de aquella tierra en anto grado quese preciaua
deme llamar y etener por hermano e haũ que le
mudase la volũtad a hoffender esta gẽte el nilos suios
nosabẽ que sean armas y andan desnudos como yahe
dicdo sõ los mas temerosos que ay en el mũdo

asiquesolamente la gente que alla queda es para
destroir toda aquella tierra y es ysla sĩpeligro de sus
personas sabieudoseregir entodas estas islas me parece
que todos los õbres sean cõtẽ tos cõ vna muger i asu
maioral o Rey dan fasta:veynte: las mugeres me
parece que trabaxã mas que los õbres ui hepodido en
tender sitenien bienes propios que me parecio ver ǫ a
ǫllo que vno tenia todos hazian parte en especial
delas cosas comederas en estas islas fasta aqui no
hehallado õbres mostrudos cõmo muchos pensauan
mas antes estoda gẽte demuy lindo acatamiento ni sõ
negros como ẽ guinea saluo cõ sus cabellos corredios
ynosecrian adõdeay ĩpeto demasiado delos rayos
solares es verdad quel sol tiene alli grand fuerca
puesto que esdi distinta dela liña ĩqui nocial veĩte
eseis grãdes en estas islas adõdeay mõtñas grandes:ay
tenia a fuerca el frio este yuierno:masellos lo sufren
porla costumbre que cõla ayuda delas viandas comen
cõ especias muchas y muy calientes endemasia:asique
mostruos nohe hallado ninoti cia saluo de vnaysla que
es aqui enla segunda ala eutrada delas yndias ǫ es
poblada devna iente que tieuẽ en todas las yslas por
muy ferozes los qualles comẽ carne vmana estos tienẽ
muchas canaus cõlas quales corrẽ todas las yslas de
ĩdia robã ytomã quanto pneden ellos no sõ mas
difformes que los otros saluo ǫ tienẽ encostumbre
detraer los cabellos largoscom omugeres y vsan arcos
y flechas delas mismas armas decañas cõ vn palillo
alcabo pordefec to de fierro ǫ no tienẽ sõ ferozes
eutre estos otros pneblosque sõ ẽdemasiado grado
couardes mas yo no los tengo en nada mas que
alos:otros estos sõ aquellos ǫ tratã cõlas mugeres
dematremonio ǫ es laprimera ysla partiendo despaña
para las ĩdias ǫ se falla enla qual no ay
hõbrenĩguuo:ellas uo vsã exercio femenil saluo arcos y
frechas como los sobre dichos de cañas ysearman y
cobigan cõlaunes de arambre deque tienẽ mucho otra

ysla meseguran mayor q̃ la española euque las psouas
no tienẽ ningũ cabello En esta ay oro sĩ cuento y
destas y delas o tras traigo comigo ĩdios para
testimonio:e cõclusiõ afablar desto solamẽte quesea
fecho este viageque fueasi de corida que puedẽ versus
altezas q̃yo les dare oro quanto ouiẽrẽ menester con
muy poquita ayuda q̃ sus altezas medarã agora
speciaria y algodõ quãto sus altezas mãdarã cargar y
almastica quauta mandaran cargar e:dela qual fasta oy
no seha fallado saluo en gre cia enla ysla de xio y el
señorio la uende como quiere y liguñaloe quãto
mandaran cargar y es clauos quãtos mãdaran cargar e
seran:delos ydolatres y creo hauer fallado ruybaruo y
caue la e otras mil cosas desustancia fallare que
hauran fallado la gẽte que yo alla dexo porque yo
nomehe detenido nĩgũ cabo en quãto eluiento me aia
dado lugar:denauegar solamente en la villa de nauidad
enquanto dexe aseguardo E bien asẽtado E ala verdad
mucho mas ficiera si los nauios me siruieran como
razõ demandaua Esto es harto y eterno dios n nestro
señor el qual da a todos aquellos q̃ andan sucamino
victoria de cosas que parecen imposibles:yesta
señaladamẽte fuela vna por q̃ haũ que destas tierras
aian fallado O escripto todo va por cõ lectura sin
allegar deuista saluo cõprendiendo a tanto que los
oyẽtes los mas escuchauan e iuzgauan mas por fabla
quepor poca [cosa] dello asi que pues nuestro:
Redemtor dio esta. vic toria A nuestros Yllustrisimos
rey:ereyna eas [us] reynos Famosos d[et]ã alta cosa A

dõde toda La christiandad deue tomar alegriay fazer
grandes fiestasy dar gracias solẽnes ala sancta tri
nidad cõ muchas oraciones solẽnes por el tanto en
xalcamiento que hauran en tornando se tantos
pueblos a nuestra sancta fe:y despues por los bienes
tẽpora'ls q̃ no solamẽte ala españa mas atodos los
christianos ternan aqui refrigerio y ganancia esto
segun el fecho asi embreue fecha enla calauera sobre
las yslas de canaria a xv de febrero año Mil.
cccclxxxxiii.

Fara lo que mandareys   El Almirãte

Anima que venia dentro en la Carta

Despues desta escripto:y estãdo en mar de. Castilla
salio tanto viẽto cõ migo.sul y sueste que me ha fecho
descargar los nauios po cori aqui en este puerto
delisbona oy que fue la mayor marauilla del mundo
adõde acorde escriuir asus altezas. entodaslas yndias
he siempre halla do los tẽporals como en mayo adõde
yo fuy en xxxiiidias y volui en xxviii saluo questas
tormen tas me ãde tenido xiiii dias corriendo por esta
mar:dizen aqua todos los hõbres dela marq̃ia mas ouo
tan mal yuierno no ni tantas perdidas de naues fecha
ba quatorze dias de marzo:

ESTA Carta en bio Colom A'escriuano Deraciõ
Delas Yslas Halladas en Las Yndias:Cõtenida
A Otra De Sus Altezas

The Barcelona Letter of 1493

TRANSLATION FROM THE SPANISH

BY LUCIA GRAVES

SIR: BECAUSE I KNOW you will take pleasure in the great victory that Our Lord has given me in my voyage, I write this letter to inform you of how in twenty days I reached the Indies with the fleet supplied to me by the most illustrious King and Queen, our Sovereigns, and how there I discovered a great many islands inhabited by people without number: and of them all I have taken possession on behalf of Their Highnesses by proclamation and with the royal flag extended, and I was not opposed. I named the first island I found San Salvador, in commemoration of His Divine Majesty, who so wonderfully has created all this: the Indians call it Guanaham. The second I named Santa María de Concepción; the third Ferrandina; the fourth Isabella, the fifth Juana Island; and so to each a new name.

When I reached Juana I followed its coast westward and found it so large that I thought it might be terra firma, the province of Cathay. I did not discover in this manner any towns or villages along the coast, only small hamlets whose inhabitants I could not speak to because they all fled at our sight, but I continued on that route, not wanting to miss any great city or town. After many leagues there was still no change, and the coast was leading me north, where it was not my wish to go, because winter had set in and I wanted to avoid it and go south; moreover, I had a head wind, so I decided not to wait for better weather and turned back to a large harbor, whence I sent two men inland to find out whether there was a king or any big cities. They walked for three days and discovered an infinite number of little villages and countless people, but no such thing as a government; for which reason they returned.

It was made clear to me, by other Indians whom I had captured earlier, that this entire land was an island; so I followed its coast eastward for one hundred and seven leagues until it came to an end, and from that cape I saw another island to the east, eighteen leagues away, which I later named La Española, and there I went. I sailed eastward along its northern coast, as I had done in Juana, covering 178 long leagues in a straight line. This island and all the other ones are exceedingly grandiose, and this one in the extreme. There are harbors on the coastline that cannot be compared to any others I know in all Christendom, and plenty of good large rivers that are a marvel to see. Its lands are high and have a great many sierras and soaring mountains, unmatched by those of the island of Tenerife, for they are indeed all very beautiful, and of a thousand different shapes, and accessible, and full of all kinds of trees, so tall they seem to touch the sky; I have heard it said, moreover, that these trees never lose their leaves, which I can well believe, for I saw they were as green and beautiful as they are in Spain in the month of May. Some were in blossom, others with fruit, others yet at a different stage, according to variety; and I could hear nightingales and other small birds of a thousand different kinds singing in the month of November, wherever I went. There are six or eight kinds of palm tree which are a wonder to behold on account of their beautiful and unusual shapes, and the same can be said of the other trees, fruits and plants. On this island there are marvelous pine woods and vast fields; and there is honey, and many kinds of birds and a great diversity of fruits. This land also has many mines of metal, and people in uncountable number.

La Española is a marvel. Its sierras and mountains, its lowlands and meadows and its beautiful thick soil, are so apt for planting and sowing, for raising all kinds of cattle and for building towns and villages. As for the seaports here, seeing is believing; and so also the many big rivers of good water, most of which carry gold. The trees, fruits and plants are very different from those of

Juana: in this island there are many spices and great mines of gold and other metals.

The people of this island, and of all the other islands I have found or heard about, go naked, men and women alike, just as their mothers bear them, although some women cover one single place with a leaf or with a piece of cotton which they make for this purpose. They have no iron or steel or weapons, nor are they inclined to such things. This is not from lack of vigor or handsome build, but because they are unbelievably fearful. Their only arms are canes, cut when in seed, with a sharp stick attached to the end, but they dare not use them: for it often came to pass that I would send two or three men ashore to some village to talk with its dwellers, and crowds would stream out towards them, but upon seeing our men at close quarters they would turn around and flee, parents not even waiting for their children. This was not because any harm had been done to any of them; on the contrary, in every place I have visited and have been able to talk with the people, I have given them of all I had, such as cloth and many other things, receiving nothing in return; but they are just hopelessly timorous. True it is that once they feel reassured and lose this fear they are then so guileless and generous with what they have that one would not believe it without seeing it. If you ask them for something they have, they never say no; instead, they offer it to you with such love that they would give you their very hearts. Then, whether their gift was of great or little value, they are happy to receive any little trifle in return.

I forbade that they be given such worthless things as pieces of broken bowls, or pieces of broken glass, or lace-tags, although when they could obtain any of these, they considered it the most precious jewel in the world. It happened once that a sailor received the weight of two and a half *castellanos* in gold for a lace-tag; and others, for other things that were worth even less, received even more. For newly coined *blancas* those people would give all they had, even two or three *castellanos'* weight in gold, or a quarter or two of spun cotton. They even accepted broken hoops of wine casks, and like fools gave all they had for them. That seemed wrong to me, so I forbade it and I gave them sundry good things that I brought with me so as to gain their love and, moreover, that they might become Christians, for they are inclined to love and serve Their Highnesses and the whole of the Castilian nation; and they endeavor to gather and give us things which they have in abundance and which are necessary to us. They did not know any sect or idolatry, except that they all believe that power and goodness abide in heaven. Indeed, they believed very firmly that I with these ships and people came from heaven, and with corresponding regard they received me in every place, once they had lost their fear. And this is not because they are ignorant, for they have a very subtle ingeniousness and travel all over those seas, it being a wonder to listen to the good accounts they give of everything, but because they had never before seen people wearing clothes, or ships like ours.

When I arrived in the Indies, I took some of these people by force in the first island I found, so that they might learn our language and give me news of what existed in those parts. And so it happened, for later they understood us and we them, either by speech or by signs: and they have been very useful to us. I am bringing them with me now, and they still think I come from heaven, despite all the conversation they have had with me. These were the first to announce it wherever I went; others would run from house to house and to nearby villages shouting, "Come! Come and see the people from heaven!" Thus they all, men and women, old and young, once their hearts were sure of us, would come out, leaving no one behind, and each bringing something to eat and drink which they gave to us with wondrous good will.

In all these islands there are very many canoes, similar to longboats, some of which are large and others smaller, many being even larger than a longboat of eighteen benches; but not as wide, for they are made of a single piece of timber. A longboat, however, could not keep up with them with oars alone, for they go with incredible speed. With these canoes they travel all over those islands, which are innumerable, and ply their merchandise. I have seen some of those canoes with 70 or 80 men aboard, and each with his oar.

In all these islands I did not see much diversity in the people's features, or in the customs, or in their language. What is more, they all understand each other, which is a remarkable thing, and for that reason I hope that Their Highnesses will decide on the preaching to them of our Holy Faith, to which they are very well disposed.

I have already related how I traveled 107 leagues along the coast of Juana, following a straight line from west to east. Accordingly, I can say that this island is larger than England and Scotland together: for beyond those 107 leagues there are two provinces on the west side which I have not visited. One of them is called Auan, where people are born with tails. These provinces must be at least fifty or sixty leagues long, or so I understand from the Indians I have with me, who know all these islands.

This other island called Española has a circumference greater than the whole of Spain from Colunya all along the coastline up to Fuenterrabía, in Biscay: for I followed one of its quarters in a straight line from west to east and covered 188 long leagues. This island is to be coveted; and once seen, one would never leave it. Since I have taken possession of all these islands for Their Highnesses, and since they are all richer than I know or can say, I hold them all on behalf of Their Highnesses, who can dispose of them in the same way and just as fully as the very kingdoms of Castile. In Española I have taken possession of a large town, which I have named Villa de Navidad. It is situated in the most convenient spot on the island and in the best district for gold mines and for all kinds of trade with the nearest mainland as well as with the farther one of the Great Khan, where there will be much commerce and gain. In this town I have built fortifications which by now must be entirely completed, and I have left enough men there for the purpose, with arms and artillery and victuals for over a year; also a longboat and a master seaman skilled in all the arts for building more; and I have great friendship with the king of that land, to such a degree that he took pride in calling me his brother and treating me as such. But even if he were to change his mind and act against my men, neither he nor his people know anything about weapons, and go around naked, as I have said: they are the most faint-hearted people in the world, and the few men I have left behind would suffice to destroy the whole of that land. The island offers no danger to their lives as long as they know how to govern it.

In all these islands it seems to me that men are content with one woman, and they give their chief or king up to twenty. Women work more than men, it seems to me, but I have not been able to ascertain whether these people have any private belongings, for I think I saw that what one had was shared by all, especially food.

Until now I have not found any monstrous men in these islands, as many had thought. On the contrary, all these people are very good-looking: they are not black as in Guinea, but have flowing hair, and they do not make their homes in places where the rays of the sun are too strong. Indeed, the sun is very powerful there, being only twenty-six degrees distant from the equator. Where there are high mountains in these islands, it was intensely cold this winter, but they are able to endure it, by habit and with the aid of the many exceeding hot spices which they eat with their food.

So, I have found no monsters nor had any news of any, except from one island, the second one at the entrance to the Indies. It is inhabited by a people who are considered in all the other islands to be extremely fierce, and who eat human flesh. These people have many canoes with which they have the run of all the islands of the Indies; they steal and take all they can. They are no more deformed than the rest, and can only be distinguished from them because they have a habit of keeping their hair long, like women, and use bows and arrows, made of the same canes as the weapons I described earlier, with a stick on the tip instead of iron, which they do not have. They are ferocious when compared to the other islanders, who are cowardly in the extreme; but I am no more afraid of them than of the rest. These are the ones who trade with the women of Matremonio, the first island one reaches on the voyage from Spain to the Indies, and in which there lives not a single man. They are not used to feminine occupations, but carry bows and arrows, likewise made with canes, and they arm and cover themselves with plates of copper, of which they have plenty. I have been assured that there is another island larger than Española where the people are entirely bald. It abounds in gold, and I bring Indians with me from this and the other islands to testify to it.

In conclusion, to speak only of what has been done on this hasty voyage, Their Highnesses can see that I will give them as much gold as they may need, with but a little help from Their Highnesses. Also spices and cotton, as much as Their Highnesses order me to load; and as much mastic as they order loaded, which until now had been found only in Greece on the island of Chios and which the Seignory sell for the asking. They can also have as much aloe as they order loaded, and as many slaves as they order loaded, who will be idolaters. I also think I have found rhubarb and cinnamon, and I will find a thousand other things of substance which the people I have left behind will have discovered. For I have not tarried anywhere when the wind allowed me to sail, except in the Villa de Navidad, which I left secured and well settled. And, truly, I would have done much more if the ships had served me as it would have been reasonable to expect.

This is enough, and Eternal be God our Lord, who grants, to all those who walk in His path, victories over things that appear impossible. And indeed this was a great victory, for even though people may have spoken and written about these lands, all was conjecture, nobody actually having seen them. It amounted to this: that most of those who heard these stories listened, but judged them rather from hearsay than from the least bit of proof. Thus our Redeemer has granted victory in so great a matter to our most Illustrious King and Queen, and to their renowned kingdoms. For which the whole of Christendom should rejoice and make merry, giving solemn thanks to the Holy Trinity, with many a solemn prayer, for all the glory they will receive when so many peoples turn to our Holy Faith; as well as for the temporal benefits, which will bring renewal and gain not only to Spain but to all Christians.

This, in brief, according to the facts. Written on board the caravel, by the islands of Canary, on February 15 of the year 1493.

At your orders. The Admiral

Nema that came inside the letter:

After this letter was written, being within the seas of Castile, I met with such strong south and southeast winds that I was forced to unload the ships. But today I was driven into this port of Lisbon, an event which was the greatest marvel in the world, and here I have decided to write to Their Highnesses. In all the Indies I have always found the weather to be like that of the month of May. I went there in 33 days and returned in 28, save that these storms have detained me 14 days tossing about the sea. Here all the seamen say that there was never so bad a winter nor such a great loss of ships. Written on the fourteenth day of March.

This letter Columbus sent to the Secretary of the Treasury about the Islands Discovered in the Indies. Contained in another to Their Highnesses.

NOTES ON THE TRANSLATION

RINTED WITH OBVIOUS HASTE, the Barcelona Letter is riddled with typographical errors, compounded by senseless letter- and word-spacing and by the lack of punctuation and paragraphing. Thus the punctuation and paragraphing of the translation are moot: Their main object is to reflect as closely as possible the eccentric rhythm and grammar of Columbus' Spanish. Holes in the original (indicated with brackets in the transcription) have been filled with sensible guesses. Passages that require comment are listed below.

PARAGRAPH 1

". . . how in twenty days I reached the Indies . . ." Actually 33 days, as stated in the postscript.

PARAGRAPH 3

"Tenerife": misspelled *cētre frei* in the original.

PARAGRAPH 6

"castellanos": Large gold coins.

"blancas": copper coins akin to pennies.

". . . a quarter or two of spun cotton": i.e., 25 pounds per quarter.

PARAGRAPH 10

"Auan": the Havana region of Cuba.

PARAGRAPH 11

"Since I have taken possession of all these islands . . ." This passage seems to have been mangled on press. The bottom line on page 2 of the pamphlet did not register clearly, and was repeated in slightly different language at the top of page 3.

PARAGRAPH 13

". . . twenty-six degrees distant from the equator": actually, 21 degrees.

PARAGRAPH 14

"Matremonio": Martinique.

PARAGRAPH 15

"Seignory": the government of Genoa.

PARAGRAPH 17

". . . by the islands of Canary . . ." Actually, the Azores.

PARAGRAPH 19

"Anima" or *nema:* postscript on a separate sheet.

". . . southeast winds . . ." Actually, southwest.

". . . on the fourteenth day of March." Actually, the 4th.

PARAGRAPH 20

"Contained in another . . ." Referring to the *nema* itself contained in the letter.

MAP OF THE WORLD BY
JUAN DE LA COSA

MAPPAMUNDI BY JUAN DE LA COSA, C. 1500 (INK AND COLOR ON OXHIDE, 175 × 96.5 CM., MUSEO NAVAL, MADRID).

This is the earliest known map to incorporate "the Indies," which by then were being systematically explored but not yet recognized as a separate continent. La Cosa confusingly highlighted the American portion by depicting it on a much larger scale than the Old World, but he rendered the Caribbean in particular with impressive accuracy. The author of this spectacular map was the same Juan de la Cosa who was the owner and maestre *of the* Santa María *and who sailed with Columbus on the first two voyages.*

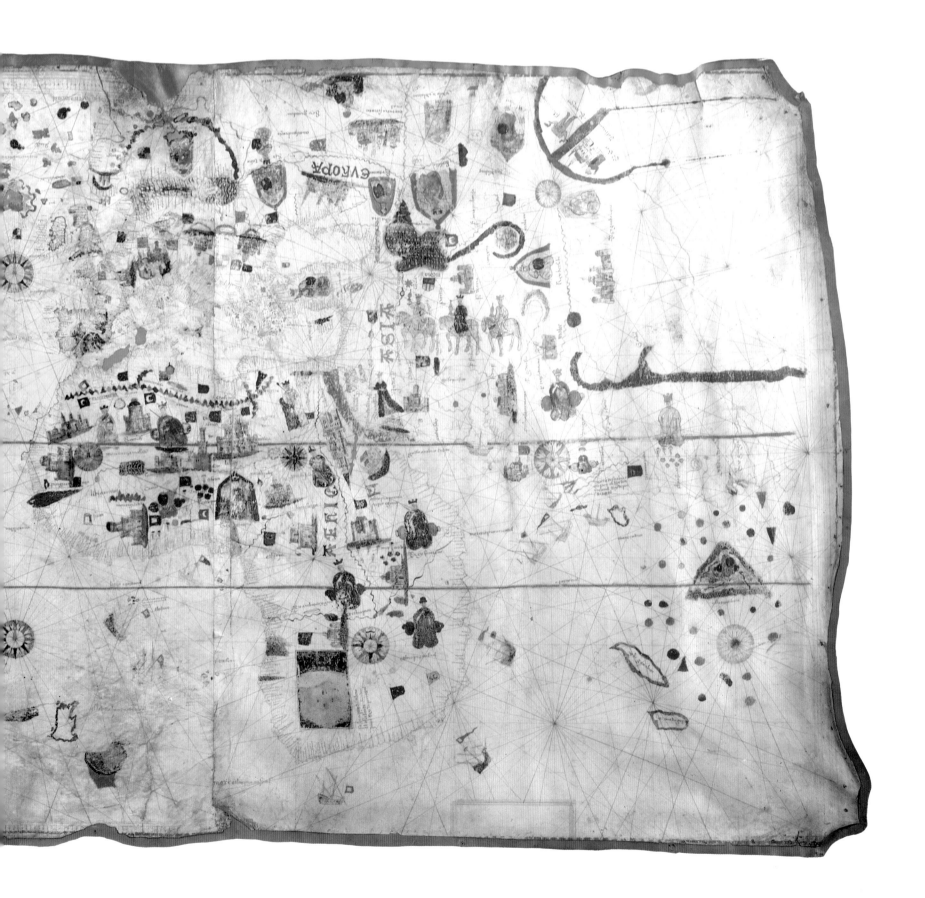

CHRONOLOGY OF COLUMBUS' FIRST TRANSATLANTIC VOYAGE

FTER OBTAINING his *Capitulaciones* from Ferdinand and Isabella in the spring of 1492, Columbus spent three months preparing his fleet at Palos, on the Atlantic coast of Andalucia. His crew of about 90—mostly Spaniards, with a handful of foreigners—included two medics, a tailor, a jeweler, various shipwrights and other essential craftsmen, and a scholar expert in Oriental languages as interpreter, but no clergy or women, since this was purely a scouting expedition. Following is a chronology of the voyage based on the Journal.

AUGUST 3, 1492	Departure of the fleet from Palos half an hour before sunrise.
AUGUST 12	Arrival in the Canary Islands. Almost one month spent in the Canaries making repairs and stocking new provisions.
SEPTEMBER 8	Beginning of transatlantic crossing on westward course before dawn.
SEPTEMBER 14	Two birds blown aboard, thought to be sign of land.
SEPTEMBER 16	Arrival in Sargasso Sea, also mistaken by crew as sign of land.
SEPTEMBER 25	False sighting of land from the *Pinta*. Columbus changes course to southwest.
SEPTEMBER 26	When no land appears, Columbus changes back to original course.
OCTOBER 7	Second false sighting, but Columbus notes flocks of birds flying southwest and again changes course.
OCTOBER 10	The crew, already restive, "could stand it no longer." Columbus attempts to cheer them on, but feels obliged to promise to turn back if land is not sighted within a few days.
OCTOBER 11	Worst gale of the crossing further frightens the men, but a floating branch with a flower still attached, and other definite proofs of land, lift spirits.
	One hour before moonrise, about 10 PM: First sighting of a flickering light in the distance.
OCTOBER 12	*About 2 AM:* First sighting of land by Rodrigo de Triana, lookout on the *Pinta.* Columbus decides to wait until daylight before approaching the shore.
	Just after daybreak: First landing, on Guanahaní, in the Bahamas, of which Columbus takes possession for the Spanish Crown and which he names San Salvador.
OCTOBER 15	Discovery of Santa María de Concepción (now Rum Cay).
OCTOBER 16	Discovery of Fernandina (Long Island).
OCTOBER 19	Discovery of Isabella (Crooked Island).
OCTOBER 28	Discovery of Cuba, which Columbus names Juana. He explores the northern coast for more than a month.
NOVEMBER 22	Martín Alonso Pinzón absconds with

the *Pinta* on independent search for gold.

DECEMBER 6 — Discovery of Española.

DECEMBER 7 — Indian jewelry on Española first evidence of substantial supply of gold.

DECEMBER 24–25 — The *Santa María* is wrecked on a reef off northern Española. Columbus decides to build the fort of Navidad.

JANUARY 6, 1493 — The *Pinta* rejoins the *Niña.*

JANUARY 16 — Three hours before daybreak, with Columbus on the *Niña,* the two caravels begin the return voyage to Spain. Diego de Arana and 39 men are left behind in Navidad.

FEBRUARY 13–14 — A terrifying storm separates the *Pinta* and the *Niña.* Columbus hastily writes a short relation of the voyage on a piece of parchment and orders it thrown overboard in a coffer.

FEBRUARY 18 — Arrival of the *Niña* in Santa María in the Azores. During a week of bickering with the Portuguese governor, half the *Niña's* crew are arrested, then set free.

FEBRUARY 23 — Departure from the Azores on the course for Spain.

FEBRUARY 26 — A cyclone overtakes the *Niña* and for a week drives her directly toward Lisbon.

MARCH 4 — Arrival in Lisbon harbor at about 9 AM. Columbus dispatches his report on the voyage to the Secretary of the Treasury, Luis de Santángel, his backer at the Spanish court.

MARCH 13 — After ten days of polite detention and questioning by the Portuguese, departure for Palos.

MARCH 15 — Arrival in Palos. Meanwhile, Pinzón has arrived in northern Spain and requested interviews at Court independently, and been refused.

AROUND MARCH 30 — Letter published in Barcelona by Pedro Posa.

AFTER APRIL 7 — Columbus receives letter from Court dated March 30 addressing him as "Admiral of the Ocean Sea, Viceroy and Governor of the islands he has discovered in the Indies," inviting him to come to Court and requesting that he arrange to prepare a second voyage as soon as possible.

END OF APRIL — *Recepción triunfal* of Columbus at Court, in Barcelona's Tinell Palace.

SEPTEMBER 25 — Departure of second voyage from Cádiz, with 17 ships and 1200–1500 crew and colonizers.

MAURICIO OBREGÓN, historian, engineer, navigator, flyer, underwater archaeologist, and diplomat, is today's foremost authority on the voyages of the great discoverers. For fifteen years he worked with Samuel Eliot Morison tracing the routes of Columbus, Magellan, and the Vikings, among others. Later he continued his research by sea and by air, and also retraced the *Odyssey* and the argonautica. He has served as an Overseer of Harvard University and as President of the University of the Andes in Bogotá, where he now holds the Chair of History of Discovery.

Among Mr. Obregón's writings in English are *The Caribbean as Columbus Saw It* (with Morison), *Ulysses Airborne, Argonauts to Astronauts,* and "The Rise of Islam" in *The Practical Stylist.*

LUCIA GRAVES read Spanish at Oxford and has translated many books between English and Spanish, including titles by Robert Graves, Rafael Alberti, and Anaïs Nin. Her latest translation into English is Pardo-Vasán's *The House of Ulloa* (Penguin Classics). Ms. Graves lives in the mountains of northern Majorca.

THE TEXT OF THIS BOOK HAS BEEN TYPESET BY AMERICOMP,
BRATTLEBORO, VERMONT, IN SIMONCINI GARAMOND,
AN ITALIAN VERSION OF CLAUDE GARAMOND'S ROMAIN
DE L'UNIVERSITE, DESIGNED BY F. SIMONCINI AND W. BILZ
IN 1958 IN COOPERATION WITH LUDWIG & MAYER. THE
DISPLAY HAS BEEN TYPESET ON A MACINTOSH COMPUTER
USING ADOBE GARAMOND, DESIGNED BY ROBERT SLIMBACH
IN 1989.

THIS EDITION WAS PRINTED ON PHOENIX-IMPERIAL HALBMATT
(170 GSM) BY A. MONDADORI IN VERONA, ITALY.

PRODUCTION MANAGEMENT BY CAMILLO LOGIUDICE
DESIGN BY JANET TINGEY